Literary Criticism and Cultural Theory

The Interaction of Text and Society

Edited by
William E. Cain
Professor of English, Wellesley College

A Garland Series

Postcolonial Masquerades

Culture and Politics in Literature, Film, Video, and Photography

Niti Sampat Patel

Garland Publishing, Inc.
New York and London
2001

Published in 2001 by
Garland Publishing Inc.
29 West 35th Street
New York, NY 10001

Garland is an imprint of the Taylor & Francis Group

The author and publisher gratefully acknowledge the permission of the following to reproduce the illustrations in this book: figures 1 and 2, BFI Films: Stills, Posters and Designs and Channel 4 TV; figures 3 and 4, Women Make Movies; figures 5, 6, 7, 8, and 9, Jean Mohr.

10 9 8 7 6 5 4 3 2 1

Library of Congress Cataloging-in-Publication Data
Sampat Patel, Niti.
    Postcolonial masquerades : culture and politics in literature, film, video, and photography / Niti Sampat-Patel.
        p. cm. — (Literary criticism and cultural theory)
    Includes bibliographical references and and index.
    ISBN 0-8153-3649-7 (alk. paper)
    1. Mass media and culture. 2. Postcolonialism. I. Title. II. Series.
P94.6.S264 2000
302.23—dc21   00-042950

Printed on acid-free, 250-year-life paper
Manufactured in the United States of America

For Saurin

Contents

List of Illustrations

Acknowledgments

I am grateful to many for their advice, encouragement, and friendship. The evolution of this book owes a personal debt to many people and places. In New York, I would first of all like to thank Una Chaudhuri who served as director for this project in its dissertation stage, and Jeffrey Spear whose support and encouragement I could always count on. I am also deeply indebted to my friend and colleague Jude Rawle Ganesh for his critical and enthusiastic response to my work. I am also very grateful to Garland Publishing, particularly Damon Zucca, William Cain and all the anonymous readers and editors of my manuscript.

In Dallas, I would like to especially thank my friends, Jaina and Raghu Sanga for their support and their faith in the value of my work, and for what I hope will continue to be an enduring and stimulating friendship.

In San Diego and Boston, I wish to thank Suren Dutia, Jas Grewal, Samir Bhatia, Sushma and Mukesh Patel for their unconditional generosity and hospitality.

In London, I would like to extend a special thanks to Pratibha Parmar who gave me the opportunity to visit with her, and for her generosity in lending me all those hard to get videos that proved invaluable for my work. I would also like to thank my family in Purley and Kshitish Nadgauda and Aditi Shankar in New York for their help and hospitality. A special word of gratitude to the Women Make Movies Collective in New York, the British Film Institute and Channel 4 TV in London, for enabling me to use their resources. I am also indebted to Jean Mohr in Geneva for allowing me to use his photographs.

Additionally, I would like to acknowledge the crucial influence of the Groundwork Collective at the University of California, San Diego where I spent some very important years of my life. I learned much from my work and comrades at Groundwork, particularly the importance of forging a relationship between theoretical enterprises and hands on activism. I can only remember my days at Groundwork with fondness.

To my friends and family in India and elsewhere, I owe a special debt of gratitude. They have been a deep source of sustenance. To all my parents-Kamal and Chandrakant Sampat, Hansa and Vijay Sampat, Bhanuben and Dr. Manubhai Patel I owe a debt of gratitude that is hard to repay. A word of gratitude to Dr. J.C. Patel for his interest in, and encouragement of, my intellectual pursuits. To my sisters-Amita and Brinda, and my brother-Rajiv, I can only thank you for your love and support. Special thanks to Rajeev Kothari and Janhavi Apte-Kothari for lighting up the darker moments of my dislocation (s).

Finally, I would like to express my gratitude and dedicate my book to Saurin Patel for all his patience, steady support, and love, to our lovely daughter Maya who has brought joy in to our lives, and to the memory of Sarla masi and Rena Grant.

Introduction

In that uncertainty lurks the white-masked black man; and from such ambivalent
identification—black skin, white masks—it is possible, I believe, to redeem the
pathos of cultural confusion into a strategy of political subversion.[1]

Does (masquerade) serve primarily to conceal or repress a pregiven femininity, a
feminine desire which would establish an insubordinate alterity to the masculine
subject and expose the necessary failure of masculinity? Or is masquerade the
means by which femininity itself is established, the exclusionary practice of identity
formation in which the masculine is effectively excluded and instated as outside of a
feminine gendered position?[2]

In a postcolonial context the problematic of **masquerade** becomes a significant
site for raising questions about representation, identity, historicity, power, and
subversion. The object of this study is not to identify a consistent meaning of
masquerade, because postcolonial masquerade cannot be considered to be a
singular term, but a strategy that is profoundly heterogeneous. Figurations of
masquerade in different postcolonial contexts denote a plurality of effects and
employ a variety of strategies and are engendered differently by different social,
political, and narrative circumstances at particular moments. And, since this work
has benefited from the existence of multiple theoretical, fictional, filmic, and
photographical elaborations of masquerade, and draws from the rich plurality of
material that already exists on the subject; it ultimately challenges the assumption
that masquerade is a monolithic strategy of subversion.

Therefore, by considering a specific and different strategy of masquerade in
each chapter, I contend that each situation of masquerade expresses a different and
distinct range of conflicts and collaborations. The purpose of selecting four different
situations of masquerade is to challenge perceptions of a single, consistent,
univocal oversimplification of a strategy that I consider to be infinitely plural and

whose contradictions mark precisely the moments of instability within any postcolonial situation. It is through a consideration of this multiplicity that I interpret or read my texts and in discussing these different moments of masquerade, I attempt to locate some of the urgent questions of postcoloniality— questions of home and exile, gender identity and subversion, subalternity, translation, historicity, hegemony and resistance, activism, community building and peace.

These questions demand more than just a theoretical elaboration and signal the importance of resisting a totalizing framework that grants authority or privilege to any single 'model' of masquerade; for masquerade is multi-toned, it can be both subversive and non-subversive, critical and non-critical, ambiguous and non-ambiguous.

I attempt to explore some of the theoretical and political ambiguities of different masquerades in order to claim that they offer very useful ways to read different postcolonialities and understand different structures of hegemony that have been generated over the years. Masquerade, in my study, takes shape within very different contexts and genres—theory, fiction, film, video, and photography, and by tracing their intersection with issues of class, nationality, gender, and sexuality I wish to emphasize that representation is fundamentally heterogeneous and unequal. Furthermore, different discursive apparatuses display modes of representation differently. Yet, despite their nonequivalence, these modes do overlap and are mutually implicated in one another at different times. For this reason my ultimate aim is not to pluralize postcolonialism through these different moments of masquerade, but to *articulate* dynamic ways of reading, understanding and participating in cultural, academic, and political processes by emphasizing that relationships of inequality cannot be reduced to binary antagonisms like race and nation. However, by opening up spaces that permit *other* differences (class, gender, sexual preference) that are themselves contradictory, continuously changing, even incompatible; I wish to foreground the complexity of the task of articulating and unmasking postcolonialities. All these questions arise, in various ways, in the chapters that follow. But, it is first necessary to provide a context from which postcolonial masquerade emerges.

I would like to begin with a discussion of Frantz Fanon's concept of the mask and move on to read Homi Bhabha's concept of "mimicry". Following this I would like to elaborate a relationship between subalternity and masquerade, and masquerade and questions of sexual identity by reading the theories of masquerade in the work of Joan Riviere, Judith Butler and Jacques Lacan and film theorist Mary Ann Doane.

SITUATING MASQUERADE:

The social and psychic representation of the colonial "other" is the subject of Frantz Fanon's *Black Skin White Masks* where he poses the enigmatic and existential question: "What does the black man want?"[3] Thus, Fanon ironically turns the European existential and psychoanalytic traditions to face the history of the colonized subject that they had never contemplated.

However, the analysis Fanon undertakes is psychological even though he admits that the alienation of the black man does involve recognition of social and economic realities. Fanon's study, then, is primarily clinical and rarely historicizes the colonial experience. Bhabha writes:

> There is no master narrative or realist perspective that provides a background of social and historical facts against which emerge the problems of the individual or collective psyche. . . . The colonial subject is always "overdetermined from without," Fanon writes. It is through image and fantasy—those orders that figure transgressively on the borders of history and the unconscious—that Fanon most profoundly evokes the colonial condition.[4]

In articulating colonial and cultural alienation, Fanon uses the psychoanalytic language of demand and desire. Through the central motif of the "mask" Fanon describes the black man's desire to overcome his state of "blackness" or inferiority. He does this not by imitating the mannerisms of "whiteness" but by adopting the language of dominance as well. He writes that "every colonized people—in other words, every people in whose soul an inferiority complex has been created by the death and burial of its local cultural authority—finds itself face to face with the language of the civilizing nation; that is, with the culture of the mother country. The colonized is elevated above his jungle status in proportion to his adoption of the mother country's cultural standards. He becomes whiter as he renounces "his blackness, his jungle" (*Black Skin*, 18). The black man's confrontation with whiteness is automatically pathological and takes the form of mimicry. This mimicry is characteristic of both sexes and Fanon devotes a separate chapter to each, making his analysis center around literary texts in both cases. For Fanon, a psychoanalytic understanding of masquerade hinges on a close analysis of the realm of sexuality. In fact, Fanon's book organizes its investigation of the exotic and erotic, colonialism and racism through the various permutations in the relations between black men and white women, black women and white men, black men and white men. However, he chooses to overlook the relations between black women and white women.

With reference to the woman of color and the white man, Fanon uses the autobiographical text of Mayotte Capecia (although there are references to a short story "Nini" by Abdoulaye Sadji) to claim that most black women think it their duty to "whiten the race" by engaging in sexual relations with white men. Fanon is relentless in his critique of Mayotte, a woman from Martinique, who swears that she would never marry a black man. Fanon writes:

> Something remarkable must have happened on the day when the white man declared his love for the mulatto. There was recognition, incorporation into a group that had seemed hermetic. The psychological minus value, this feeling of insignificance and its corollary, the impossibility of reaching the light, totally vanished. From one day to the next, the mulatto went from the class of slaves to that of masters. She was recognized through her over-compensating behavior. She was no longer the woman who wanted to be white; she was white.[5]

It is through the Negresses' feeling of inferiority and desire to gain admittance into the white world that she submits to the white man. The black woman's act of masquerade, according to Fanon, is essentially an act of submission. Furthermore, she is trapped within this desire because even though Fanon raises the question of there being other possibilities for Nini and Mayotte, he quickly discards these options by referring them as "pseudo-questions" that do not concern him. If the trope signaling the colored woman's masquerade is submission, the trope that characterizes the black man's relation with the white woman is that of possession. Fanon writes:

> Out of the blackest part of my soul, across the zebra striping of my mind, surges this desire of my mind to be *white*. I wish to be acknowledged not as *black* but as white . . . who but a white woman can do this for me? By loving me she proves that I am worthy of white love. I am loved like a white man. I am a white man . . . I marry white culture, white beauty, white whiteness. When my restless hands caress those white breasts, they grasp white civilization and dignity and make them mine.[6]

Fanon's rendition of the black man's desire to claim his white identity through the sexualized possession of white woman's bodies echoes the desires of Saladin Chamcha and Gibreel Farishta in Salman Rushdie's novel *The Satanic Verses* . By analyzing the neuroses of Jean Venuse, the central character in a novel by Rene Maran, Fanon objectifies women's bodies into sites for self-definition. Like Chamcha and Gibreel, Venuse wishes to escape his race by marrying a white woman. Yet, Venuse needs authorization or sanction from the white man to do this, because Negroes have only one desire when they land in Europe—gratification from white women, and he knows that they do not marry for love, but to derive satisfaction from the thought that they are masters of white women. This, Fanon points out, is a source of conflict for Venuse and moves on to excuse Venuse's desire to possess white women by claiming that the essence of his attitude is "not to love in order to avoid being abandoned" (*Black Skin*, 76).

If the black woman's masquerade is submission and the black man's masquerade is possession, then where does the possibility of subversion lie? For the black man it takes place in the form of conquering white women's bodies, but for the black woman, in Fanon's description, there is no opportunity to resist. And because Fanon offers a notion of self/other relationships in binary terms—self as opposed to other, his masquerade is limited in its capacity to offer any radical method of resistance.

In fact, the woman of color becomes an example of the inevitable impotence of desire to be "white" (although she seems to be more at home in the realm of mimicry); whereas, through his mental traumas and conflicting emotions, Jean Venuse is able to attain a form of whiteness in Fanon's schema. However, while Fanon asks few questions of the black man's violent confrontation with women's bodies, he effectively erases the black woman's historical role by asking no questions about her.

If Fanon's masquerade hinges on a binary conception of sexuality, Homi Bhabha's notion of "mimicry" describes colonial relations in more dynamic terms even though it echoes both the psychoanalytic traditions of Fanon himself, as well as the legacies of Freud and Jacques Lacan. According to Bhabha mimicry "emerges as one of the most elusive and effective strategies of colonial power and knowledge" (*Location*, 85) because colonial mimicry is generated by a desire for a reformed, recognizable Other, ". . . as a subject of a difference that is almost the same, but not quite" (*Location,* 86). However, Bhabha points out, the discourse of mimicry is almost always constructed around an ambivalence. In his essay, "Of Mimicry and Man", in which Bhabha first introduces and elaborates the notion of mimicry, he writes:

> . . . in order to be effective, mimicry must continually produce its slippage, its
> excess, its difference. The authority of that mode of colonial discourse that I have
> called mimicry is therefore stricken by an indeterminacy: mimicry emerges as the
> representation of a difference that is itself a process of disavowal. Mimicry is thus
> the sign of a double articulation; a complex strategy of reform, regulation and

discipline, which 'appropriates' the other as it visualizes power, intensifies surveillance, and poses an imminent threat to both 'normalized' knowledges and disciplinary powers.

The effect of mimicry on the authority is profound and disturbing. . . . It is from this area between mimicry and mockery, where the reforming, civilizing mission is threatened by the displacing gaze of its disciplinary double, that my instances of colonial imitation come. What they all share is a discursive process by which the excess or slippage produced by the *ambivalence* of mimicry (almost the same *but not quite*) does not merely 'rupture' the discourse, but becomes transformed into an uncertainty . . .[7]

Thus, Bhabha identifies mimicry and ambivalence to be the primary indicators of dissonance implicit in western discourse. Mimicry offers Bhabha the possibility of constructing the colonial Other, the colonial subject who will be recognized to be the same as the colonizer—but still different. The mimic man in this case, is therefore, white but not quite. He only constitutes a partial representation for the other and far from reasserting the foundation of power that the colonizer *imagines* himself to possess, the colonized subject, through imitation subverts and undermines the absoluteness and fixity of the colonialist's authority— the very basis of his identity:

It is a process by which the look of surveillance returns as the displacing gaze of the disciplined, where the observer becomes the observed and the 'partial' representation rearticulates the whole notion of *identity* and alienates it from its essence . . .[8]

Thus, mimicry both enables power and signals a loss of agency by simultaneously stabilizing and destabilizing the position of power. However, Bhabha takes great pains to assert that mimicry does not conceal a presence or identity behind its mask. The *menace* of mimicry is its ". . . double vision, which in disclosing the ambivalence of colonial discourse also disrupts its authority. And it is a double vision that is a result of what I've described as the partial representation/ recognition of the colonial object" (*Location*, 88). However, the desire of colonial mimicry need not necessarily have an object, even though it may have "strategic objectives" that Bhabha refers to but does not attempt to explicate, as "the *metonymy* of presence'" mimicry becomes an erratic, eccentric strategy of authority in colonial discourse. The effect, however, Bhabha suggests is to question the authorization of colonial representations particularly his conceptualization of the colonial subject as an *object* of regulatory power.

Bhabha moves on to discuss the ambivalence of mimicry in terms of the Freudian fetish. He writes:

> The ambivalence of mimicry—almost but not quite—suggests that the fetishized colonial culture is potentially and strategically an insurgent counter-appeal. What I have called its 'identity effects' are always crucially *split.* Under cover of camouflage, mimicry, like the fetish, is a part-object that radically revalues the normative knowledges of the priority of race, writing, history. For the fetish mimes the forms of authority at the point at which it deauthorizes them. Similarly, mimicry rearticulates presence in terms of its 'otherness', that which it disavows...The colonial discourse that articulates an *interdictory* otherness is precisely the 'other scene' of this nineteenth century European desire for an authentic historical consciousness...the disturbance of splitting that violates the rational, enlightened claims of its enunciatory modality. The ambivalence of colonial authority repeatedly turns from *mimicry*—a difference that is almost nothing but not quite—to *menace*— a difference that is almost total but not quite. And in that other scene of colonial power, where history turns to farce and presence to 'a part' can be seen the twin figures of narcissism and paranoia that repeat furiously, uncontrollably.[9]

What Bhabha means here is that in the articulation of the authority of the cultural fetish, in the attempt to produce colonial mimicry, the identity of the colonizer is hollowed and less stably re-formed. The identity of the colonized is concurrently destabilized as mimesis or mask of the European original. in its strategic failure to discipline, mimicry is both resemblance and menace—a supplement or sly mockery of authority which reveals the fundamental inadequacy and ambivalence of European authority.

If Bhabha's concern is to demonstrate an ambivalence in colonial authority as a result of mimicry, his attempt to deal with the question of anticolonialist resistance is contained within his concept of 'hybridity'. In his essay, "Signs Taken for Wonders," mimicry is displaced by hybridity and hybridity becomes Bhabha's answer to the question of resistance because it is, for Bhabha, "a *problematic* of colonial representation . . . that reverses the effects of colonial disavowal, so that the other 'denied' knowledges enter upon the dominant discourse and estrange the basis of its authority" (*Critical,* 156). Thus, hybridization subverts colonial authority by opening up spaces for other marginalized and repressed kinds of knowledges to effect a transformation. The returning gaze of hybridity not only produces an unease or ambivalence of colonial authority but produces grounds for intervention:

> If the effect of colonial power is seen to be the *production* of hybridization . . . (it) enables a form of subversion . . . that turns the discursive conditions of dominance into grounds of intervention. [10]

For Bhabha, discursive conditions of colonialism do not merely undermine the forms of colonial authority but can actively enable resistance. This acknowledgement on Bhabha's part is an important theoretical advance in his own work because now mimicry is not just disquieting but has the capacity to intervene:

> Mimicry marks those moments of civil disobedience within the discipline of civility: signs of spectacular resistance. When the words of the master become the site of hybridity . . . then we may not only read between the lines but even seek to change the often coercive reality that they so lucidly contain. [11]

Bhabha's call for active resistance, however, is still a matter confined within the contours of discourse. One has to read between the lines in order to change perceptions. Also, such an intervention that Bhabha is making a claim for leaves unanswered the question of the location of agency. Who reads between the lines, when and to whom? As Robert Young points out:

> Is Bhabha describing a forgotten moment of historical resistance, or does that resistance remain inarticulate until the interpreter comes a hundred and seventy years later to 'read between the lines' and rewrite history? And precisely what reality can such a reading between the lines hope to change? Is it a question of locating previously undetected moments of pre-nationalist subaltern resistance that can now be produced and charted by the critic? [12]

Certainly Bhabha's emphasis on the act of reading does not attempt to address some of the questions concerned with location of agency. Gayatri Chakravorty Spivak has commented on this problem in her essay "Can the Subaltern Speak?" by asserting that while resistance can be accomplished in acts of (re) reading, ultimately the subaltern cannot speak by herself and be heard on her own terms. She is almost always spoken for. Spivak very aptly locates the (im) possibility of the Indian subaltern woman's agency by signaling the silencing of the subaltern woman as the point where the interpreter must acknowledge the limits of historical understanding. It is not possible to retrieve the subaltern woman's voice consciousness, for example, on its own terms when she is denied the position of subject. But this inability is not disabling because the interpreter's recognition of the limits of historical knowledge and her own ability to retrieve the "true voice" frustrates any imperialist attempt to speak on behalf of the subaltern woman. Undercutting the project of traditional, dominant historiography, Spivak is not in favor of recovering the voices of marginal women-workers, peasants, and minorities. The project of retrieval always begins at the erasure of the subaltern. Its possibility is, therefore, also its impossibility. The intervening critic/historian, therefore, must continually and persistently interrogate her/his attempts of retrieval—a problem that Bhabha continually glosses over when he speaks of any form of resistance or intervention. Spivak's understanding of the subaltern's erasure is not ultimately nihilistic and this is evident in her emphasis on community building and active organizing elaborated in her recent translation of Bengali writer Mahasweta Devi's short stories. This attempt at building communities as a way of seeking active support is the task of a very subversive mode of masquerade that I explore in the video work of British/Indian filmmaker Pratibha Parmar. By embracing masquerade as the dominant mode or technique of filmic practice Parmar forges a relationship between marginalization and masquerade. And by placing the responsibility of masquerade in the hands of subaltern women, Parmar is able to create spaces for different forms of political and cultural activism.

Several theorists, particularly in the arena of psychoanalysis and queer theory, have discussed the subversive practice of masquerade by women. One of the earliest known elaborations of female masquerade is Joan Riviere's essay "Womanliness as Masquerade," first published in 1929 in the *International Journal of Psychoanalysis*. Its context is that of the work done by analysts on sexual difference and female sexuality. However, it is not until recently that the idea of masquerade has received any attention or gained currency particularly in thinking about questions of representation, sexual difference and agency in connection with film theory.

Riviere's essay is concerned with women who wish for masculinity and who put on a mask of womanliness as a defense from the anxiety and retribution feared from men.[13] Riviere moves on to develop her idea of masquerade in terms of the castration complex and its sources in the oedipal situation. Thus the masquerading woman/patient resolves her problem through a reenactment of oedipal rivalry. So, in her successful professional career, her rivals take the place of her father and by flirting with them she placates them; "it was an unconscious attempt to ward off anxiety which would ensue on account of the reprisals she anticipated from the father-figures after her intellectual performance" (*Formations*, 37). Having exhibited herself in possession of her father's penis (through her masquerade), she castrates him and seeks refuge from his anticipated anger by offering herself as the castrated woman to other father figures. Thus, her whole life revolves around alternate masculine and feminine activities. Masquerade enables her to triumph over her parent objects. However, at the center of Riviere's paper is the question of feminine identity:

> The reader may now ask how I define womanliness or where I draw the line between genuine womanliness and the 'masquerade'. My suggestion is not, however, that there is any such difference; whether radical or superficial, they are the same thing. The capacity for womanliness was there in this woman—and one might say it exists most completely in homosexual women . . .[14]

In masquerade woman mimics authentic femininity, except that authentic femininity is itself a masquerade that continues to remake itself for Riviere. Therefore, femininity as masquerade is dissimulation of any pre-given originary identity. What, then, is masked by the masquerade? Judith Butler attempts to answer this question by posing a series of possibilities. I quote her at length:

> Is masquerade the consequence of a feminine desire that must be negated and, thus, made into a lack that nevertheless, must appear in some way? Is masquerade the consequence of a denial of this lack for the purposes of appearing to be the Phallus? Does masquerade construct femininity as the reflection of the Phallus in order to disguise bisexual possibilities that otherwise might disrupt the seamless construction of a heterosexualized femininity? Does masquerade as Riviere suggests, transform aggression and fear of reprisal into seduction and flirtation? Does it serve primarily to conceal or repress a pregiven femininity, a feminine desire which would establish an insubordinate alterity to the masculine subject and expose the necessary failure of masculinity? Or is masquerade the means by which femininity itself is *first* established, the exclusionary practice of identity formation in which the masculine is effectively excluded and instated as outside of the feminine gendered position?[15]

Lacan explores the subversive possibilities of feminine masquerade and attempts to answer the questions raised by Butler. Since Lacan refutes the primacy given to ontology by Western theory, he is more concerned with explanations of how identity is constructed through signifying practices. This is the basis of Lacan's theory of language and sexual difference where in order to appear to be the Phallus, the woman has to masquerade. But for Lacan masquerade is a contradictory act. If being the phallus is masquerade then all being becomes a form of appearance. Yet, at the same time masquerade suggests that there is a "being" prior to masquerade, a feminine desire that is masked and capable of disrupting any phallogocentric signifying practices. So masquerade can be both a performative production of sexual identity that constantly remakes itself, or a form of denial of feminine desire by presupposing a pre-existent femininity not represented by the phallic economy. However, within Lacanian terms it appears that femininity as masquerade negates any notions of pre-given, fixed identities.[16]

The question of locating agency through masquerade is examined thoroughly by Judith Butler[17] who claims that masquerade as performance opens up possibilities of agency foreclosed by positions that presuppose fixed and foundational gender identities. According to Butler being female does not constitute a natural fact. It must be understood as a cultural performance whereby gender parody does not assume that there is an original that it imitates, and "that the gendered body is performative suggests that it has no ontological status apart from the various acts which constitute its reality" (*Gender*, 136).

The idea of primary gender identity according to Butler has been parodied within many cultural practices like drag and cross-dressing which feminists have either criticized as sex-role stereotyping or an uncritical appropriation of identity, particularly in the case of butch/femme lesbian identities. But, Butler writes, "the relation between the "imitation" and the "original" is...more complicated than that critique generally allows" (*Gender*, 137). She writes:

> The performance of drag plays upon the distinction between the anatomy of the performer and the gender that is being performed. But we are actually in the presence of three contingent dimensions of significant corporeality: anatomical sex, gender identity, and gender performance. If the anatomy of the performer is already distinct from the gender of the performance, then the performance suggests a dissonance not only between sex and performance, but sex and gender, and gender and performance. As much as drag creates a unified picture of "woman" . . . it also reveals the distinctness of those aspects of gendered experience which are falsely naturalized as a unity through the regulatory fiction of heterosexual coherence. *In imitating gender, drag implicitly reveals the imitative structure of gender itself—as well as its contingency.*[18]

The subversive potential of feminine masquerade in film theory is explored in some detail by Mary Ann Doane who believes that by flaunting femininity, masquerade constructs a certain distance from it denying the production of femininity as closeness or as presence to itself. She writes "masquerade . . . involves a realignment of femininity, the recovery, or more accurately, simulation of the missing gap or distance between oneself and one's image...it is not that a man cannot use his body in this way but that he doesn't have to. To masquerade doubles representation; it is constituted by the hyperbolization of the accouterments of femininity" (Femme, 25–26).

Doane moves on to describe the experience of female spectatorship in terms of a dynamic masquerade that confounds the masculine structure of the look by destabilizing and defamiliarizing the female image and iconography. For Doane, masquerade does not merely constitute the norm of femininity as it does for Riviere and Lacan, but a way of destabilizing the image. By providing the contradiction that attributes to woman the distance and divisibility of the self rather than excessive presence, masquerade allows for the possibility of agency by designating a distance between the woman and the image of femininity.

Having provided the context for postcolonial and feminine masquerade, then, I proceed to discuss different strategies of masquerade in the chapters that follow. In chapter 1, "Unmasking Masquerade: Home and Exile in the Films of Hanif Kureishi," I explore varying positions of postcolonialities where the classic dilemma of "home" is played out in diverse ways. In both his films *My Beautiful Laundrette* and *Sammy and Rosie Get Laid* marginal characters (blacks, homosexuals, lesbians, socialists, working-class youth, women and other subcultures) co-exist in a space where belonging is contingent.

Set against the backdrop of Margaret Thatcher's London of race riots and decrepitude, Kureishi and his director Stephen Frears use masquerade to unmask the dilemmas of representation and manifestations of hegemonies by exposing the constructedness of identities and signifying practices and the multifaceted aesthetic and political meanings of Diaspora culture.

The disruptive practices of masquerade that characterize Kureishi's films become ambiguous in chapter 2, "Beyond the Rushdie Affair: Women, Masquerade and Translation in *The Satanic Verses*," where I explore Rushdie's "anxiety" about translating women into postcolonial narrative and historiography. Using Tejaswini Niranjana's theory of postcolonial translation as disruption I propose that masquerade as a strategy for translating women in Rushdie's novel is at best ambiguous if not completely ineffectual. In chapter 3, "The Voices of Masquerade: The Representation of Subalternity in Two Videos by Pratibha

Parmar," I forge a relationship between Spivak's notion of subalternity and masquerade to display that the marginalized woman can effectively use masquerade to disrupt patriarchal structures and "speak" for herself and on her own terms. Here, I ask not if the subaltern can speak, but explore the ways in which it might be possible to unmask the dilemmas of language and voice to create communities that empower subalterns to speak. We have already seen that masquerade can be an effective means of subversion for the woman. In this chapter I explore the possibilities of masquerade for the marginalized or minority woman who is often left on the fringes or outskirts of discourse to emphasize that she, too, can speak for herself and on her own terms. In the fourth and last chapter, "Photography as Mask: Edward Said's *After the Last Sky*," I discuss issues of Palestinian exile through the photographs of Palestinians taken by Jean Mohr and the theoretico-poetical narrative by Edward Said that accompanies them. Here, I discuss the photograph as the transcription of the real or the mask that both conceals and reveals what is behind it thwarting confrontation with any simplistic notions of factuality or reality. And, by juxtaposing pictures with a narrative that is both congruent and disjunctive, Said re-creates the trauma and alienation of a dispossessed people and indicates the possibility of creating communities that can provide a basis for organization and support. By forcing us to re-think questions of community, nation, and identity, Said's text challenges dominant images of Palestinians from a hybrid place where diverse modes of the personal and the political, of representation and self-representation intersect and co-exist. By unmasking the life activities of living Palestinians in exile, Said is able to mobilize and give these hitherto mute representations a voice without it becoming the "authentic" voice of alienation and exile.

This interdisciplinary study of masquerade brings together an assorted selection of texts ranging from the intensely personal to the densely theoretical to display how fiction, film, video, and photography shape notions about identities and cultures. However, the elusive nature of masquerade itself , makes it an extremely potent concept because it cannot be thought of as a generalized condition or strategy. All displaced or marginalized people do not use or experience it equally or monolithically. In fact, masquerade thrives on specificity and locality and the different strategies discussed in the chapters that follow are themselves so diverse and multifaceted that no obvious link can be established between them. And, in order to illustrate just how often and widely the theoretical category of masquerade has undergone redefinition, this study attempts to place masquerade within different frameworks. The evolutions of masquerade will, of, course continue and relocate and manifest themselves differently in an increasingly globalized world and market place. In fact masquerade is continually being redefined and modified as different political, social, and economic structures come into play. It is, therefore, a useful and dynamic concept that illustrates and critiques the impact of recent changes in technology, power, community, nationality and capital. Masquerade can also be used to empower the growing numbers of dispossessed people that are victimized and terrorized by the advent of globalization because it contains within it the potential to enable the creation of interactive communities. This is not to suggest that strategies of masquerade are inherently subversive. It is rather to suggest that such strategies can become, in specific contexts, important arenas for critical praxis.

I have attempted, through my study of masquerade, to communicate both the possibilities and the limitations of the concept. Hence, the diverse nature of the texts. For, the very nature of masquerade, in a sense, forces its own rearticulation within different contexts. As identities and nations become more complex, multiple, and contradictory, our experiences are re-shaped, and in my attempt to unmask different patterns of masquerade, I chart its various divergences and possibilities. Thus, in each chapter I discuss a specific form of masquerade (s) and suggest that each situation expresses a different and distinct range of possibilities limitations, and concerns that are not necessarily linked by any monolithic notion or model of masquerade but part of an ongoing redefinition of the term. The sheer mobility of the concept, its capacity to move beyond borders and subjectivities indicates its remarkable capacity to rearticulate the context it is derived form. Masquerade dispenses with the idea fixity even though it can invoke both an active resistance or, as in some cases, an active adherence to authority. There are all sorts of ironies within the production of masquerade (s) that make it an immensely alluring activity to understand the workings and representations of widely different postcolonialities.

My aim, in this work, then, is to bring together a set of texts in which conceptions of masquerade are articulated. While my choices of texts are artificial, one can, through them, synthesize many debates that surround the question of postcolonialism (s). This apparently arbitrary choice of texts can also display what I consider to be some of the most central cultural and political issues confronting us. In part, it reflects a need to articulate different levels of debate. My intention is to offer a progressive notion of postcolonial masquerade by suggesting the possibility of community that is a necessary prerequisite for any effective politics.

NOTES

1. Homi Bhabha, *The Location of Culture* (London and New York: Routledge, 1994) 62.

2. Judith Butler, *Gender Trouble: Feminism and the Subversion of Identity* (New York and London: Routledge, 1992) 48.

3. Fanon's question echoes Freud's famous question: "What does a woman want?"

4. Homi Bhabha, "Remembering Fanon", *Remaking History*, eds. Barbara Kruger and Phil Mariani (Seattle: Bay P, 1989) 136.

5. Frantz Fanon, *Black Skin, White Masks* (New York: Grove, 1967) 58.

6. Frantz Fanon, *Black Skin, White Masks* (New York: Grove, !967) 63.

7. Homi Bhabha, *The Location of Culture* (London and New York: Routledge, 1994) 86.

8. Homi Bhabha, "Of Mimicry and Man: The Ambivalence of Colonial Discourse," *October* 28 (1984): 129.

9. Homi Bhabha, *The Location of Culture* (London and New York: Routledge, 1994) 91.

10. Homi Bhabha, "Signs Taken as Wonders: Questions of Ambivalence and Authority Under a Tree Outside Delhi, May 1817," *Critical Inquiry* 12.1 (1985): 154.

11. Homi Bhabha, "Signs Taken for Wonders: Questions of Ambivalence and Authority under a Tree Outside Delhi, May 1817," *Critical Inquiry* 12.1 (1985); 162.

12. Robert Young, *White Mythologies: Writing History and the West* (New York: Routledge, 1990) 149.

13. The case from which Riviere develops her argument involves a successful intelligent woman who seeks reassurance from men in the form of sexual attention. See Joan Riviere, "Womanliness as Masquerade," *Formations of Fantasy*, eds. Victor Burgin, James Donald and Cora Kaplan, (London: Routledge, 1986): 35–44.

14. Joan Riviere, "Womanliness as Masquerade," *Formations of Fantasy*, eds. Victor Burgin, James Donald, and Cora Kaplan (New York: Routledge, 1986) 38.

15. Judith Butler, *Gender Trouble: Feminism and the Subversion of identity* (New York: Routledge, 1990) 47–48.

16. See Jacques Lacan, "The Meaning of the Phallus," *Feminine Sexuality* (New York: Norton, 1982).

17. Judith Butler, *Gender Trouble: Feminism and the Subversion of Identity* (New York: Routledge, 1990).

18. Judith Butler, *Gender Trouble: Feminism and the Subversion of Identity* (New York: Routledge, 1990) 137. For more information on drag, cross-dressing and masquerade see Jane Gaines and Charlotte Herzog, eds. *Fabrications: Costume and the Female Body* (New York: Routledge, 1990), and Marjorie Garber, *Vested Interests: Cross-Dressing and Cultural Anxiety* (New York: Routledge, 1992).

Postcolonial Masquerades

CHAPTER ONE

Unmasking Masquerade: Home and Exile in the Films of Hanif Kureishi

The masks of the clown grant the right to confuse, to tease, to hyperbolize life; the right to parody others while talking, the right not to be taken literally, not "to be oneself . . ." the right to rip off masks . . . [1]

The mask represents the absent one. It brings the unknown to recognition, the unrepresentable to representation. The mask itself is an object, it is abstract; yet it indicates that the content is present in abstraction—where the known becomes the unknown, the identical becomes different. The unrepresentable and unknowable is always "the missing content," that the mask recovers and brings forth. The mask puts the world upside down—it is a masquerade. [2]

. . . If we do look back, we must also do so in the knowledge—which gives rise to profound uncertainties—that our physical alienation . . . almost inevitably means that we will not be capable of reclaiming precisely the thing that was lost; that we will in short, create fictions, not actual cities or villages, but invisible ones, imaginary homelands . . . [3]

Hanif Kureishi's films *My Beautiful Laundrette* and *Sammy and Rosie Get Laid* construct varying positions of postcoloniality by displaying and displacing a wide range of discourses that intersect, reformulate, and revolve around the axis of race, class, and sexuality set against the decay of Margaret Thatcher's England. Kureishi's films also function as theoretical and social texts where questions of postcoloniality and migrancy are interrupted by the chaotic existence of other sub-classes and the movement from the one to the other makes clear that "questions of race and postcoloniality are not identical." [4]

3

In both films, the classic postcolonial/migrant dilemma—the dilemma of "home" is played out through the explosive confrontations between Asian immigrants and the different sub-classes in Britain. In many ways the presence of sub-cultures in Kureishi's films can be interpreted as responses to the growing influx of black immigrants in Britain and represents a highly neglected dimension of race relations.[5]

It is from this perspective of race, postcoloniality, migrancy, and sexuality, that I wish to examine the renegotiations of aesthetics and politics in Kureishi's films. Both *My Beautiful Laundrette* and *Sammy and Rosie Get Laid* are social texts that simulate a variety of aesthetic practices that display a highly pronounced concern not only with the politics of racism but also the politics of representation. Kureishi's films, I will argue, attempt to decolonize existing notions of filmic subject matter and practice.

In both films marginal characters (blacks, lesbians, homosexuals, working-class youth, and other outcasts) clash and co-exist in a space where there can be no absolute sense of belonging—only a contingent sense of "home". It is against this backdrop of multiple contestations of space that Kureishi/Frears **unmask** the dilemmas of representation. Kureishi's films are **dialogic** texts that use different strategies of **masquerade** to de-naturalize and expose the constructedness of signifying practices and the absurdity of reading them as fixed, stable and neutral. Here dominant cinematic codes are deconstructed by blurring the line between truth and fiction, realism and artifice. But before I move on to a detailed reading of the films, I want to, reflect on the concept of **dialogism** that I believe characterizes both Kureishi's films.

Dialogism was first formulated by Mikhail Bakhtin to describe the relation between utterances:

> Utterances are not indifferent to one another, and are not self-sufficient; they are aware of and mutually reflect one another. . . . Each utterance is filled with echoes and reverberations of other utterances to which it is related by the communality of the sphere of communication. . . . Each utterance refutes, affirms, supplements, and relies on others, presupposes them to be known, and somehow takes them into account.[6]

Extremely diverse and politically heterogeneous currents have appropriated the word dialogism, as Robert Stam points out. It is not my intention to provide an exhaustive discussion of the word. Suffice it to say that in my reading of Kureishi's films I hope to illuminate some aspects of dialogism, particularly as they relate to filmic practice. For this purpose I draw extensively from the work of Robert Stam and Kobena Mercer.[7]

Robert Stam points out that dialogism, even though it is at its root, interpersonal, it can apply by extension ". . . to the relation between languages, literatures, genres, styles, and even entire cultures . . ." (*Subversive*, 14). Furthermore, Stam points out, "Dialogism refers to the relation between the text and its others not only in relatively crude and obvious forms of argument—polemics and parody—but its much more diffuse and subtle forms that have to do with overtones, pauses, implied attitude, what is left unsaid or is to be inferred" (Subversive, 14). Bakhtin, himself, commented on these often unacknowledged forms of dialogism as "the layering upon meaning," "voice upon voice" and the "combination of voices" (*Subversive*, 14). In fact the concept of dialogism, by emphasizing the relational aspect of utterances suggests that every text forms an intersection of textual surfaces where other texts may be read. However, Stam points out that *dialogism* in Bakhtin's work progressively acquires meanings and connotations without ever losing its central idea of "the relation between the utterance and other utterances" and although Bakhtin refers to dialogue to provide examples of the dialogic, the two cannot be equated. Nor can dialogue be seen as in absolute opposition to monologue because a monologue can also be dialogic.[8]

Bakhtinian dialogism, however, is far more radical, because it appeals not just to literary and artistic traditions, but common, everyday speech as well. Stam writes:

> Dialogism operates within all cultural production, whether it be literate or nonliterate, verbal or nonverbal, highbrow or lowbrow. In the films of Godard or Ruiz, the artist becomes the orchestrator, amplifier of the ambient messages thrown up by all the series—literary, painterly, musical, cinematic, publicatory, and so on. But the same basic dialogical mechanisms also operate within what is known as "popular culture" . . . For Bakhtin . . . entire genres, languages, and cultures are susceptible to "mutual illumination". His insight takes on special relevance in a contemporary world where communication is "global", where cultural circulation, if in many respects asymmetrical, is still multivoiced, and where it is becoming more and more difficult to corral human diversity into the old categories of independent cultures and nations. Third World culture . . . is by definition a multivoiced field of intercultural discourse . . . [9]

In his essay "Diaspora Culture and the Dialogic Imagination: The Aesthetics of Independent Black Film Making," Kobena Mercer describes the two main tendencies of British filmmakers, monologic and dialogic. Underlying the monologic tendency is the filmmaker's uncritical appropriation of and dependency on the transparent language and codes of dominant culture and filmmaking. This, Mercer believes, is an instance of cultural mimicry and "neo-colonial surrender" even though their subject matter might deal with the politics of racism. They are committed to a mimetic concept of representation that assumes that reality "has an objective existence out there" and that the process of representation simply aims to correspond to or "reflect it."

On the other hand, Mercer points out, critical dialogism is a project of decolonization, "creolization," or "carnivalization" where strategies of montage and dissonance disrupt notions of a fixed and unchangeable reality. He writes, ". . . Carnival is not "the revolution," but in the carnivalesque aesthetic emerging here we may discern a mobility of what Bakhtin called the "dialogic principle" in which the possibility of *change* is prefigured in collective consciousness by the multiplication of social dialogues" (Blackframes, 56).

Thus, the dialogic tendency in Kureishi's films can be seen as disruptive. Challenging dominant filmic language and codes by entering into a dialogic relationship with the films' apparent realism, the dialogism in Kureishi's films is responsive to the diverse and complex qualities of Britishness. Furthermore, the dialogism in both *My Beautiful Laundrette* and *Sammy and Rosie Get Laid* is characterized by a highly pronounced concern with the politics of representation. By disarticulating given signs and rearticulating them in different and often contrary contexts, Kureishi's films are creative performances of the critical process of *dialogism*.

A PLACE OF RAGE: "HOME" AS MASK IN *MY BEAUTIFUL LAUNDRETTE*:

The predicament of postcolonialism and migrancy can be articulated through the problematic concept of "home" in Kureishi's first film *My Beautiful Laundrette*. There is an extremely poignant moment in this film when Omar's disillusioned father Hussein reminds his son that— "They hate us in England. And all you do is kiss their arses and think of yourself as a little Britisher!" In this scene Hussein extends the dilemma of postcoloniality to include the migrant and is careful enough to point out the **difference** between his son **thinking of himself as a Britisher** by acting like one rather than actually **being** one. And it is because of this relationship between the particularity of Omar's experience and the generality of racism in Britain that Hussein's rage and pathos is also mine, ours and everyone else's who has had to face the contradictions of inhabiting *imaginary* *homelands.*[10] Yet, postcoloniality cannot be conflated with the contradictions that inhabit diasporic space. What I mean by this is that postcoloniality is not the same as migrancy and we recognize this very important but often neglected difference in Hussein's statement. Hussein's statement for all its generality and lack of precariousness reminds us how much more complicated our relation to this "new" or adopted homeland can be. In this statement we can, to use Spivak's words, grasp the overdetermination of *both* the migrant and the diasporic postcolonial, as well as what "dominant—subordinate interraciality might mean," "It's quite often understood," Spivak points out, "as a sort of chromatic issue, as a question of skin color. It is of course very much more complicated, not (just) a cultural exchange, but a moving target based on the city—civitas (for civil-ity rather than civilization), and polis (for street politics rather than political system)" (*Outside*, 250–251). In other words, it is the explosive confrontation between cultures that dominate the streets and the inhabitants of Kureishi's inner London that one must turn to in order to understand an important aspect of dominant/subordinate race relations. The differential responses of white British youth culture to black immigrants requires a reassessment that demands a movement away from the normal areas of race-relations studies—the school, police, media, the political system—to a more complex and perhaps marginalized dimension of race and race relations—the diasporic postcolonial's encounter with the metropolis.

However, in *My Beautiful Laundrette*, Hussein's (Omar's father and Nasser's brother) and Nasser's (the wealthy Pakistani businessman and Omar's uncle) encounter with the city is not the same as Omar's, or Salim's. Hussein's postcoloniality is reflected in his nostalgic longing for a homeland and represents a dilemma very different from Omar's sense of displacement. While both father and son are marked by the same desire to reclaim a space of their own, they manage the crisis this presents in ways that are different and often incompatible.

In fact the spaces that exist in *My Beautiful Laundrette* are also different and incompatible. They are spaces where fantasy mingles with naturalism, lyricism and surreality with reality; where postcoloniality and migrancy clash with race and where ultimately the space of transgressive sexuality set against heterosexuality offers a way out of the quandaries of inter-raciality. In Kureishi's film London is a landscape where multiple notions of "home" emerge and subside— "home" as England, "home" as Pakistan/India, "home" in the midst of oppression and domination, "home" as a site of struggle for communal space, "home" as an admission of uncertainty and ambiguity, "home" as a space of contestation, racist aggression and family disintegration, "home" as a sense of loss, "home" as a place of rage and exclusion, "home" which is eventually shattered and where its appeal remains confined to the imaginary.[11]

In *My Beautiful Laundrette*, these multiple versions of "home" are presented like masks that both distort and disguise reality and "deframe" it at the same time. It is also against this background of dream and reality that the desire for a complete and uncontaminated sense of belonging arises for both the displaced postcolonial Pakistanis and the enraged white working-class youth. And it is this relationship set amidst the turmoil of Mrs. Thatcher's London that I wish to turn to in my reading of "home" in Kureishi's film. Hamid Naficy refers to this type of situation as a "crisis" whereby "Millions of people do not and cannot live in their homeland, many others are homeless within their native lands, and many of those who own houses are so afraid of what lies beyond that they have turned their dwellings into fortresses[12] (*Home*, 6).

Home as a site of turbulence and violent confrontation is established in the very first shot of the film when Salim, the wealthy Pakistani landlord and his four Jamaican companions break into a house (that supposedly belongs to Salim but has been temporarily converted into a squat) and physically evict the sleeping Johnny, Genghis, and Moose, who are the homeless representatives of a white sub-culture in Kureishi's squalid and nightmarish megapolis—London. This opening shot is the prologue of the film and provides the viewer with a frame within which the succession of confrontations between Johnny and his mates, and the Pakistani immigrants and Genghis, Moose, and their "gang", continuously disrupt the illusion of comfort and safety that the notion of "home" ordinarily suggests. In fact most of the confrontations between the gang members and the immigrants in the film are related to a desire in both parties to protect constantly threatened communal and national spaces as well as a rapidly declining status. Genghis tells Omar "to go back to the jungle" where he came from. But Salim, on the other hand, while he drinks to Thatcher and her government, claims that there is nothing left for the likes of Johnny and his gang in England because England is now the home of immigrants like himself and Nasser who know how to squeeze the system, make money, and attain "respectability":

> These People. What a waste of life, They're filthy and ignorant. They just abuse
> people. Our people. (To Johnny) All over England, Asians as you call us are
> beaten, burnt to death. Always we are intimidated. What this scum need . . . is a
> taste of their own piss. He accelerates fast, and mounting the pavement, drives at
> the LADS ahead of him. They scatter and run . . . GENGHIS gets in close against
> a wall, picking up a lump of wood to smash through the car windscreen and drops

it as SALIM drives at him . . . MOOSE is suddenly standing stranded in the centre of the road. SALIM can't avoid him. MOOSE jumps aside but SALIM drives over his foot. MOOSE screams . . . [13]

It is clear from this and other instances of antagonism and violence between the immigrants and white subcultures that a new pattern of interaction was at work in the late seventies that exploded the myth of consensus that mesmerized and characterized pre-Thatcherite government. In his essay, "The Toad in the Garden: Thatcherism among the Theorists", Stuart Hall attributes the popularity of Thatcherism to its ability to represent itself as:

> . . . a discursive formation, (that) has remained a plurality of discourses about the family, the economy, national identity, morality, crime, law, women, human nature. But precisely a certain unity has been constituted out of this diversity. [14]

The exposure of dissent and conflict at the level of working class sub-cultures reveals a crack in Thatcher's primary political project and desire for homogeneity. For clearly all was not well at home for Genghis, Moose, and their mates. Their desire to appropriate a lost community produced an intensified "Us—Them" consciousness and sense of being excluded from their own space. I believe that the "gangsters" in *My Beautiful Laundrette*, like the skinheads, dealt with their exclusion by turning to violence. John Clarke comments on the situation of the skinheads:

> Paki-bashing involved the ritual of aggressive defense of the social and cultural homogeneity of the community against its most obviously scapegoated outsiders— partly because of their particular visibility within the neighbourhood. . . . The sense of being "in the middle" of a variety of oppressive and exploitative forces produces a need for group solidarity, which though essentially defensive, in the Skinheads was coupled with an aggressive content, the expression of frustration and discontent through the attacking of scapegoated outsiders. [15]

The gangsters in Kureishi's film clearly feel oppressed by more than one authority structure; they resent people who have pretensions to social superiority and certainly successful businessmen like Salim and Nasser proclaimed themselves to be the new caretakers of an enterprise culture that had no place for "uselessness."

In a sense the conflict between the immigrants and the various youth subcultures redefined questions of national identity contesting who can and who cannot belong to the British nation. The prerequisites for belonging to the nation had shifted dramatically and in the name of the politics of diversity the new enterprise culture created a deliberate rift in the creation of alliances and solidarity. The discontent of this period was attributed to the growing influx of black immigrants who threatened the British way of life. And, the only way these immigrant groups could create a space for themselves was by exploiting the system and taking advantage of Thatcher's free market economics.[16] Nasser points this out to Omar and his friends while drinking a toast to Margaret Thatcher:

> In this damn country which we hate and love, you can get anything you want. It is
> all spread out and available. That's why I believe in England. You just have to know
> how to squeeze the tits of the system.[17]

Thus, there was a movement by some immigrants toward Thatcher's revival of free market capitalism. This realignment or fundamental regrouping of people across boundaries was typical of Thatcherism. Nasser makes money by taking advantage of what the system has to offer and both Omar and Salim are driven by a desire for upward mobility. They are able to create a space for themselves in the dominant ideology that the Left and the Labor government for all their lip service to immigrant rights were not able to provide them with. These Pakistanis worked hard to establish businesses and voted Tory. Their interests and inclinations were the same as small business owners anywhere in the world and though they were subject to more hatred and violence, particularly by other sub-classes, they wanted to elevate themselves by acquiring economic power. This they thought would make them secure. Nasser, then, "can make something out of Omar," that his brother, Omar's father, cannot. After all, as Nasser points out to Omar, "what chance would the English give a leftist, communist Pakistani" (*London*, 53)?

The constitution of Thatcherism, then, points to the consolidation of a new political language that affected a profound political/racial problem for Asian immigrants in Britain—the language of upward mobility. Stuart Hall notes that:

> Thatcherism has, in these areas, positively won space. It set out to and has
> effectively become a populist force, enlisting populist consent among significant
> sections of the dominated classes, successfully presenting itself as a force on the
> side of people and moving into a commanding position in society through a
> combination I have elsewhere characterized as 'authoritarian populism' . . . We are

looking here at a significant shift in thinking. Far from one whole unified class outlook of an opposing class, we are obliged to explain an ideology that has effectively penetrated, fractured, fragmented the territory of the dominated classes, precipitating a rupture in the traditional discourses and actively working on the discursive space, the occupancy or mastery of which alone leads it to become a leading popular ideological force.[18]

The penetration of Thatcherist ideology and the subsequent recomposition of classes resulted in the creation of deep antagonisms among the immigrant and white sub-classes. The growth of organizations like the National Front (we learn that Johnny was a part of this organization) and other right-wing groups within the subclasses resorted to violence, most notably 'paki-bashing.' Sharply differentiated by a system that encouraged frugality and the profit motive, Salim's antagonism and contempt for Johnny and his mates represents a reversal of race relations prior to the seventies and eighties where first generation immigrants shared common cultural space with their white working class neighbors. "Confirmed Anglophiles . . . they shared the same goals, the same diversions . . ." (*Subculture*, 40). However, with the advent of the second wave of immigrants, there emerged a greater sense of dissatisfaction. Dick Hebdige writes:

> For these the movement to England represented both the last ditch attempt to salvage something worthwhile from life and a 'magical' solution to their problems. Perhaps because there was less to loose, more was invested in the transition to Great Britain: hopes of an almost religious nature and intensity were pinned on the outcome.[19]

And when the outcome was scarcity of housing, loss of jobs, loss of community, general discrimination; the earlier sense of optimism and integration was lost and the only way out (as they saw it) was by making money: ". . . we're nothing in England without money" says Salim to Omar (*London, 85*).

If the existence of opportunity seemed more important to Salim, Nasser and Omar; Genghis and the lads signal the breakdown of consensus and their aggression toward the Pakistani immigrants could be read as a displacement of fear and anxiety produced by their apparent success. Less easily assimilated to the Thatcherian way of life than Salim, Omar or Nasser, their sense of belonging is threatened. This is evident in Genghis' conversation with Johnny:

GENGHIS: Why are you working for them? For these people? You were with us once. For England. JOHNNY: It's work, I want to work. I'm fed up of hanging about. GENGHIS: I'm angry. I don't like to see one of our men groveling to Pakis. They came here to work for us. That's why we brought them over. OK? . . . Don't cut yourself off from your own people. Because there is no one else who wants you. Everyone has to belong.[20]

"Everyone has to belong," seem to be the crucial words here. For all of Genghis and his mates' violence seem to be hopeless attempts to reclaim a lost sense of community and territory. Even Johnny who leaves his friends to work for Omar is marked by the desire to reclaim what was once theirs; "JOHNNY: (indicating OMAR) We were once like that" (*London*, 44).

However, for all their desperate attempts to regain their sense of home, Genghis and Moose cannot revive a sense of community that the previous generation once had. Instead, they use an *image* of what their community once was—an emblem of a certain working class tradition, to create a false sense of security by sharing the same prejudices that their parents and grandparents had toward immigrants and aliens. However, they do this without adhering to any kind of work ethic or any complete sense of belonging. For Moose and Genghis' sense of belonging is provisional like Johnny's and Nasser's and Hussein's and everyone else's. Ironically they share this sense of imagined community with their Pakistani counterparts and to a great extent the sense of toughness and masculinity adopted by them characterizes their need to adopt certain common elements of style that could foster at least a provisional sense of belonging. Ultimately, Genghis' and Moose's aggressiveness toward Salim and the other Pakistanis represents what Hebdige refers to as a 'frozen dialectic' that is "incapable of renewal, trapped, as it is, within its own history, imprisoned within its own irreducible antimonies" (*Subculture*,70).

Perhaps Hussein and Nasser are also trapped within this 'frozen dialectic.' Given their general unpreparedness to give up an 'idea' of home that they brought with them, they too are prisoners of their history. Hussein, it seems represents the position of 'failed radicalism' in *My Beautiful Laundrette*. Drunk and without a job, this once very successful socialist journalist occupies a vital place in Kureishi's film—he signals one of the many crises of postcoloniality—what Milan Kundera refers to as ". . . the struggle of memory against forgetting." Having been displaced culturally he has not learnt to accept the provisional nature of all truths and certainties. Haunted by his sense of equality and idealism Hussein believes that education is still the road to power. He wants to send his son to university and cannot understand why Omar would want to get together with a former fascist and make money-cleaning underpants:

> PAPA: Don't get too involved with that crook. You've got to study. We are under siege by the white man. For us education is power.[21]

Plagued by racial tension, Hussein recognizes England's growing economic problems:

> PAPA: This damn country has done us in. That's why I'm like this. We should be there. Home.[22]

But Nasser disagrees with his brother and believes that economic motives alone determine the nature of "home":

> NASSER: But that country has been sodomized by religion. It is beginning to interfere with the making of money. Compared with everywhere, it is a little heaven here.[23]

Nasser understands the extent to which he is formed by England and harbors no illusions about going back to Pakistan. Although his own life is submerged in the sordid reality of racial hatred, his desire to see himself succeed economically leads him to cling to the British ideals of secularism that were completely denied by the Islamization of Pakistan. Yet, despite everything Nasser cannot escape Pakistan. His own "home" crumbles before him when his superstitious wife threatens to caste an evil spell on his English mistress and resolves to go back to Pakistan, and when his daughter decides that she, too, cannot stay in the midst of family turmoil and leaves "home."

For Hussein the dilemma is different. The lack of possibility in Pakistan leads him to pursue his intellectual and political ideals in England where he encounters a society eroded by racial tension and a new enterprise culture of moneymaking. This lack of possibility in his adopted "home" leaves him in a perpetual state of limbo. Hussein cannot embrace England as "home" anymore, and even though he wishes he were back in Pakistan it is clear that Hussein is in a permanent state of exile. In England Pakistan would just not go away. Thus, even though Nasser and Hussein want to escape Pakistan completely and forever; they still cling to an *idea* of their homeland that they are not able to give up. This sense of contingency or provisional belonging is worn like a mask where the mask always marks the absent one, "*where the known becomes the unknown, the identical becomes different. The unrepresentable and the unknowable is always "the missing content," that the mask recovers and brings forth. The mask puts the world upside down—it is a masquerade*" (Blackframes, 72). How much disappointment and uncertainty might be involved in such a masquerade is evident in the extent to which both Hussein and Nasser await return to a "better" place. Hussein dreams about Pakistan, and Nasser, recognizing the extent to which he is formed by England, believes that despite everything he can and will belong. This is the diasporic condition, for the alternative to belonging is self-hatred, continuous struggles against racism in a drug infested, riot—torn, selfish, and uncaring society.

However, within the context of this very same riot—torn, racially separated society is a space that represents a reversal, a reconfiguration or inversion of dramatic space. This is the space shared by Omar and Johnny. Gayatri Chakravorty Spivak remarks that theirs is the only space that is romanticized in the film:

> In *My Beautiful Laundrette* the inter—raciality was presented in a very lyrical way between the Pakistani boy and Day-Lewis and the gay love had all the kind of erotic furniture that one associates with romantic heterosexual love . . . Of course it was a good political point because it was *still a gay thing* . . . [24]

I want to focus a little on the representation of gayness in *My Beautiful Laundrette* and suggest that by choosing to "resolve" the dilemma of "home" and interraciality through transgressive, masculine love, Kureishi makes a deliberately radical and provocative move. For Johnny and Omar are mostly *outside* the ironic framework of the film. Set against the impotent and failed heterosexual relationships in the film, their love and friendship signals, if not a common, at least a shared space. Kurieshi's political vision crystallized in Johnny and Omar is strikingly different from the murky, shadowy, and confused places inhabited by the Pakistani migrants and other sub-classes in the film. To propagate a notion of security and belonging by conflating race and transgressive sexuality in a very uncontaminated, even "pure" sense is a very bold step taken by Kureishi. Also, by providing this lyrical and even didactic relationship, both Johnny and Omar are allegorized to the extent that their relationship redefines both heterosexuality and bi-culturalism through transgression. In a certain sense Johnny and Omar have prepared us to see the fragility of fixed notions of love and inter-raciality. Theirs is a relationship that uses codes of conventional love and courtship to appropriate and rearticulate new forms of political identities and alliances. Moreover, Johnny and Omar's relationship introduces race into the vocabulary of male desire, and desirability is enhanced precisely because there exists an eroticized incompatibility between them. And it is through this process of coming together— "communifying" that Johnny and Omar are able to put aside their own private and political conflicts.

For, Omar's conflicts are not the same as Nasser's or Hussein's or Johnny's. His love for Johnny is commingled with a deeply driven desire to succeed. Unable to identify with his Uncle Nasser's, and Salim's ties to Pakistan, or with the pitfalls of his father's idealism, Omar is able to put behind Johnny's past affiliations with right-wing organizations. Johnny, too, represents an inversion of domestic space. For, Johnny disrupts the notion of community set up by his mates. His identification with the Pakistani work ethic and rejection of community as a site of contestation puts him on the outskirts of white working-class subculture and Genghis reminds him of this:

GENGHIS: Why are you working for them? For these people? You were with us once. For England. JOHNNY: It's work. I want to work. I am fed up of hanging about. GENGHIS: I'm angry. I don't like to see one of our men groveling to Pakis. They came here to work for us. That's why we brought them over. OK? Don't cut yourself off from your own people. Because there is no one else who really wants you. Everyone has to belong.[25]

Ultimately, Johnny is beaten up by his own people because he doesn't choose to fight them. The film ends with Johnny and Omar splashing water at each other—an enactment of a "cleansing ritual" or a "performative body politics,"[26] or simply a form of pleasure that refutes the notion of the body as a site for exploitation, violence and oppression, and affirms it as a site of resistance, transcendence and desire. Kenneth Kaleta comments on the film's portrayal of love:

Johnny and Omar are not only controversial bed partners, they actively assert their sexuality . . . Their involvement exists against all odds in terms of gender, race, and class . . . The political and racial conflicts Omar and Johnny confront are illuminated in their sexual encounters. As Kureishi explains, "If a black and white couple are screwing, it involves color, class, and relations between the sexes. Human relations are meeting points for a whole complex of social arrangements, and that's why I like to write about them." . . . My Beautiful Laundrette is really a story of hope, a true romance.[27]

Male homosexual desire in *My Beautiful Laundrette* also signals a crucial step forward in the direction of the film's radical aesthetic practice for two important reasons. First, because it symbolizes a new threshold of aesthetic and cultural struggle in the realm of black filmmaking in England. Second, the transgressive relationship between Johnny and Omar necessitates a discussion of how aesthetic practices in Kureishi's film have been injected with *materiality*. For it is through these signifying practices that Kureishi is able to comment on the contradictory codes of film language. *My Beautiful Laundrette* is not just about two gay men who fall in love and open a laundrette in the midst of a racially torn London; it is also about filmic practice and the constructedness of representation itself. And this constitutes the film's *materiality—it's political praxis.* To illuminate this materiality, I would like to draw on Teshome Gabriel's notion of *"the screen as mask."*

Teshome Gabriel proposes the concept of *"the screen as mask"* as an effective means of restructuring our viewing habits. This notion articulates the idea of film as *performance* where the barriers between performer-audience are both broken down and merged:

> The screen is like a painted mask . . . The screen tends to distort reality and disguises meaning, while the mask deframes the world, in inverted order, not to conceal but to heighten and add significance. The "missing content" of the screen is *"ideology"* while that of the mask is *"screen."* In both there is an exchange between absent-present and between representable-unrepresentable, except that with the screen, one does not control it; "meaning" is spelled out to us; we have no contact with the screen; it does not have the social/collective aspects of the mask. There is no social boundary with the mask. [28]

According to Gabriel the scope of the screen is limited because it frames the world for the viewer who is almost always excluded from it. "It serves as a canvas on which the West paints its own stereotypes of others" (*Out There*, 405). However, the mask has innumerable and infinite possibilities. It has an absent content both inside and outside of it, a **memory** that allows the ghosts of other histories and struggles to infiltrate and puncture the dominant histories and codes of filmic practice. To view the screen like a mask brings out the film's unstated potential, its subversiveness, its ability to redirect, even decolonize existing practices by creating new positions for beleaguered subjects and cultures.

In *My Beautiful Laundrette* the dialectic of race and sexuality is rendered doubly critical through a **dialogic** filmic strategy that does not simply resolve antagonisms but allows them to enter, exist within spaces that are constantly vigilant to the complexities of contradiction. In the end Johnny and Omar acknowledge each other's contradictions by affirming their desire, and their pleasure is a possible way to negotiate the quandaries of racial and sexual prejudice.

The element of playfulness that marks the end of Kureishi's film and characterizes the space occupied by Johnny and Omar in the film forms a subtext that runs through the entire film. For Johnny and Omar construct new forms of political identities and imagined communities. They provide the "missing content" of the film—the liberated space where racial, sexual, aesthetic and generic boundaries are demolished; they are the masks through which we can read the other spaces in the film.

In fact it is possible to read the entire filmic practice in *My Beautiful Laundrette* as a dialogue between "realism" or naturalism and the film's non-natural or "non-realistic" spaces. The film is both realistic and not realistic. It reflects both the fears and the ecstasies of Thatcherite England. Julian Henriques sums up the contradictions and struggles of *Laundrette*:

> . . . But if reality is contradictory, if we feel different feelings at the same time (funny and serious, for example), if at any one moment we can appreciate opposite forces at work, then the language of realism breaks down. For realism except in its use of irony, parody, etc., a thing cannot be one thing and another thing at the same time. But this is exactly what life is like. *Laundrette* spins round the multiple contradiction of a love affair between two men, two races, two politic.[29]

In the contradictory world of *Laundrette*, the spaces occupied by Johnny and Omar point toward the possibility of change:

> . . . It is only when reality is taken as being full of contradictory tendencies and forces, where at one moment one has the upper hand and at another the other is in ascendancy, that there can be any place for struggle . . . [30]

And this struggle is clearly at work in the film's multilayered interwoven texture of fact and fantasy. In fact *My Beautiful Laundrette's* "realism" is a discourse disguised as *histoire* that fools the viewer into believing that the film is an unmediated "natural" representation of life in the mid-1980's England. If we look closely at some of the "realistic" scenes in Kureishi/Frears's film; the scenes of decayed London at the beginning of the film, shots of Hussein's dilapidated

London flat, and glimpses of immigrant life depicted in Nasser's suburban home or Salim's decadent life of "drugs, booze, and porno films;" we notice that they are characterized by a technique typical of documentary films whereby a transparent and accurate relationship between reality and what is represented is assumed.

The film begins with a scene of eviction where Salim and the Jamaicans throw Johnny and his friends out of a decrepit London home. The camera slowly tracks to Hussein's apartment in inner London and faithfully documents its filth and neglect. Characterized by slow, tracking camera movements, these first shots in *My Beautiful Laundrette* provide us with glimpses of the squalor of urban life in England. Being entirely descriptive, the camera pauses on Omar washing clothes and making soup for his alcoholic father. His father, Hussein, pours himself a drink and chats with his rich brother Nasser on the phone, as a train rambles by. These shots recall the sordid social and economic problems of immigrant life in a very immediate, detailed, and unmediated way. For example, the camera frames a detail—a framed photograph of an English woman, (supposedly Omar's English mother) and moves on to enlarge its frame by including shots of Hussein drinking and Omar mopping the floor. Or, at another time, the camera pauses as it focuses on Hussein as he pours himself a drink from a half empty bottle which is then situated in a wider locale as the camera cuts rather unobtrusively to a shot of Omar hanging clothes in the balcony as the train roars by.

The directness of these opening shots have alarmingly led many of the film's critics to evaluate it solely on the basis of realism. Norman Stone comments on the effect of Kureishi's films:

> They are all very depressing, and are no doubt meant to be. The rain pours down; skinheads beat people up; there are race riots; there are drug fixes in squalid corners . . .[31]

While it is a fact that *My Beautiful Laundrette* is a grim rendition of urban decay, the appeal of the film lies precisely in its *break* with the realist tradition. Even when the film assumes a singular correspondence between what is represented and what actually exists in life, the film stirs up disturbing images that illustrate the inadequacy of realism for coming to terms with contemporary issues. Take, for example, the scene when Omar first visits his uncle's suburban home:

1. Omar enters his uncle's home and rings the bell. The camera pans across the drawing room as Bilquis, Nasser's wife introduces him to her guests.

2. The camera pauses as Cherry, Salim's wife, talks to Omar about his family, "home", England and Pakistan. This initiates a brief shot-reverse-shot sequence before Omar moves towards Nasser's room followed by a point-of-view shot as Cherry disapprovingly watches Tania disappear with Omar.
3. Point-of-view shot of Tania looking back defiantly at Cherry as she leads Omar to her father's room.

These scenes are interesting because they deliberately refuse variety. The frames lack depth and there is very little variation of camera angle or distance within the shot-reverse-shot stretch. In fact there is an overwhelming sense of camera presence as the characters are given little or virtually no liberties and are made to appear as if they are completely manipulated by the camera. The "reality-effect" produced by these camera movements is **mimetic** or imitative by virtue of their dependence on the four characteristic values of realism—transparency, immediacy, authority, and authenticity. However, if we move on to the scenes that follow—in Nasser's bedroom, we are made aware of the extent to which the film's realism is compromised, parodied, even caricatured:

1. The camera shifts to focus on Nasser and his drinking buddies (seen through the cracks of an opening door) as they laugh at and discuss Hussein. There is music in the background.
2. The camera slowly pans across all the men as they talk, laugh, and drink, till it pauses on Tania yawning at Omar through the back window. Now there is a distance between the camera and the men sitting around Nasser giving the frame some depth or three dimensional effect as we look at Tania in the background, the men, and Omar in the foreground looking at Tania as he converses with Nasser's friends.
3. There are a series of point-of-view shots between Omar and Nasser as they discuss Hussein's socialism.
4. The camera pans across the other men as they discuss issues of race, socialism, and communism and then cuts to Tania baring her breasts through the back window.

The sequence is remarkable not only because it is able to create a sense of depth by some camera manipulation but because it parodies, undercuts, and caricatures the "serious", male conversation by foregrounding Tania's outrageous act. The moment of comedy is rendered ironic when Zaki attributes the vision of the half-naked Tania to a *tromp d' oeil* caused by his drunken stupor. And, Cherry's discourse on "home", and sense of belonging and everything that precedes this sequence is rendered comical, and a **"false vision"** by Tania's act of defiance. Julian Henriques comments on the film's break with the realist tradition:

> The souped-up laundrette and the rest of the film were to me a fantasy expressing the feelings, contradictions, and imagination of the characters, rather than any attempt to reflect reality. In this light the mother's casting dead mice into a magic potion and the daughter's baring her breasts through the window are nothing to do with what might or might not actually happen. In fact such events might never occur in reality, but this does not make them any less real.[32]

Many of the scenes set in Nasser, Hussein, and Salim's homes only **appear** to be overtly faithful renditions of immigrant life in England because they are constantly undercut by the tragi-comic failure of the characters' ability to create a sense of belonging. Thus, in the words of Homi Bhabha, ". . . the intimate recesses of domestic space become sites for history's most intricate invasions. In that displacement the border between home and the world becomes confused; and uncannily, the private and the public become part of each other, forcing upon us a vision that is as divided as it is disorienting . . ." (*Social Text*, 141). Also, the stirring of this **"homely unhomeliness"**[33] is continuously disrupted by another world, a darker, more subterranean world where home does not remain a segment of domestic life, nor does the world become its social or historical counterpart. This is the home of Johnny, Genghis and their mates. They form what Kureishi refers to as "the gangster element" in the film and the aura of dream and fantasy that characterizes these scenes serve as a metalanguage that prevents the film's overt references to realism to claim any complete and authoritative access to truth.

These "gangster scenes" flaunt a spatial omnipresence whereby filmic space is constructed dynamically and the presentation of information is facilitated or blocked by the film's representation of space. Thus, by creating a stylized mood and texture that gives the impression that unlike the shots in Nasser's or Hussein's homes we are not in a pre-existent space, but in an abstract, recreated space where fantasy mingles with reality to create ambivalence and disjunction of political existence. These are the "unhomely" moments in the film and their effect is to traumatize any fixed notion of life that the film may have given so far. If we look closely at the scene right after Omar's first visit to his uncle, Nasser's home, when he drives the drunken Salim and his wife Cherry back home in their car, we notice a dramatic difference in the film's style and movement. Genghis, Johnny, and their friends stop their car:

1. Omar, Salim and Cherry drive off into the night. There is a point of view shot as the camera pauses on Bilquis as she stands alone by the door and watches.
2. There is music in the background as the camera cuts on to a glittering scene of London by night. A train rushes by as the camera pauses on a parked police car.
3. The camera cuts to Omar driving the car.
4. There is a point of view shot as Omar turns backwards as if in anticipation of trouble.
5. The car stops at a traffic light as Genghis and his mates close in on the three passengers. The gangster's faces are pressed against the windows as they make faces and tease the passengers.
6. There is a series of quick shots as the camera moves back and forth between the grotesque faces of the lads and the terrified Salim and Cherry.
7. Omar looks outside the side mirror and sees Johnny.
8. There is a long shot as the camera pans in on Johnny standing alone, against the graffitied wall and flickering lights.
9. Omar gets out of the car unafraid and walks toward Johnny as the lads watch, confused. The music takes on a lyrical note as Omar talks to Johnny. The camera cuts to Cherry and Salim as they ask Omar to hurry back. Omar ignores them.
10. A close up of Genghis against the shadows of the night as he watches Johnny and Omar.
11. The frame is enlarged as the camera tilts backwards to include Genghis and his friends as they move in and surround Omar and Johnny. Both are still oblivious and unconcerned.
12. Omar walks back to the car.
13. The camera cuts on to Hussein's flat and pauses as Hussein sways on the balcony. He appears as a mere shadow.

Taken collectively, these shots function to "derealize" scenic space by interjecting a romantic encounter between Johnny and Omar into a potentially violent moment. There is a lot of frame mobility in these scenes as the camera zooms in and out and as the texture and depth of the filmic space is constantly stylized by the deliberate play between light and shadow effects. The constant movement of the camera and the characters as well as unexpected frame entrances heighten spatial dissonance and create tension among the characters that the early shot-reverse-shot sequences at Nasser's house did not. In fact frame mobility is set up as the camera creates a play between onscreen and offscreen space. For example, the opening moments of the sequence sets up a comprehensive view of the locale—south London by night. However, most of the shots that follow begin on one section of the space and other aspects of space are revealed gradually. This practice is disorienting only because it engages in unexpected frame entrances. This is particularly true when the scenes of potential racial violence are interrupted by the encounter between Johnny and Omar.

Johnny's entrance into the frame signals that a different set of cues is at work in the film. The shot begins with Omar walking towards Johnny. The music changes from the rhythmic staccato sounds of suspense and anticipation that characterize the preceding shots (typical in gangster films) to the softer, lyrical notes of romantic encounter. The camera remains relatively still as Omar and Johnny talk about themselves, their families and plan to work together in the future. However, even when the camera focuses on Johnny and Omar, who are completely involved with each other, and oblivious of their surroundings; the off-screen space heralded by the lurking shadows of Genghis and his friends, remind us of the ominous discord of the earlier scenes and contaminate the lyricism of Johnny and Omar's encounter.

As Johnny and Omar talk, the camera slowly tilts backwards and enlarges their space by focusing on the flickering lights and lurking shadows in the background. Eventually the frame is enlarged as Genghis and his gang slowly moves in and encloses the private space of Johnny and Omar. Thus, the private space of the to be lovers is invaded twice, by the yelling Pakistanis asking Omar to return to the car and by a solitary close up of Genghis as he watches them through the shadows.

This constant interplay between public and private, deep and shallow spaces send confused and mixed signals that function to denaturalize filmic space because we are never able to get a singular all—embracing view of the world and are therefore not able to situate any of the figures on a cognitive map. In fact the intersection between the camera and the characters in these scenes is never linear. Even when the camera tracks Omar walking towards Johnny along a straight path and pauses for a few seconds as the two characters talk; the stillness of the frame is constantly interrupted by lingering shadows creating a spatial flux.

The constant camera movements and optical transformations are once again present in the scene where the public and private moments merge and "gangster element' is once again commingled with the codes of romantic love. When Johnny and Omar return from Nasser's home, Johnny is confronted by his mates who accuse him of abandoning them in favor of the Pakistanis. When Genghis reminds Johnny that by leaving his friends he has also given up a sense of belonging and that every one must belong, the camera, ironically, cuts to a private scene between Omar and Johnny as they exchange a kiss in the car, against a brilliant and bright full moon. Here Kurieshi/Frears's biggest challenge to realism is their use of color.

Although color is not always a challenge to realism, in *My Beautiful Laundrette* the ideological and stylized use of color suggests two possibilities; pleasure/terror and spectacle and fantasy.

In the gangster scenes there is not only a significant play between shadow, darkness and light, but the warm colors that situate and set Johnny apart from his mates are continuously mingled with the cold tones of blue and white. These are particularly predominant in the scene where Johnny confronts his mates. The first shot between Johnny and Omar is shot in soft focus and in a diffused and somewhat hazy white. When Johnny meets Genghis and the lads, the soft focus gives way to an illuminated background of white and blue that hurts the eye, until, we move on to the next frame with Johnny and Omar, where the same blue and white colors are retained, but in softer, more diffused tones.

Functionally, the non-natural use of color and the intermingling of styles and traditions in these sequences is more concerned with negotiating a certain kind of unease that increases as the film moves away from realism and a stylized technique becomes more prominent. This is particularly evident in the "laundrette sequence" that occurs on the day Johnny and Omar inaugurate their new and refurbished laundrette. This sequence is the start of the denouement of the film when the film adopts a more artificial or "constructed" mode. The shot sequences are shorter, there is more camera movement characterized by harsher, more abrupt cuts or "enjambments" as the relationships between the characters unfold and all heterosexual relationships breakdown. Nasser is abandoned both by his wife and his mistress, and his daughter, Tania, leaves home. Hussein is left longing for a pure and uncontaminated "home", and Genghis and his mates beat up Salim. The only space that is left sacred and untouched in the film is the one occupied by Johnny and Omar. This is the space of the laundrette—"Powders"—a space set apart from the brutal world of London. And, even though this space is touched by violence of urban subcultural discord, it is also a space where love is consummated and realized.

The entire "laundrette sequence" is shot with a soft focus lens as the camera slowly tracks the delicate, pastel yellow walls painted with fluffy blue and white clouds. This is the space where Kureishi/Frears counterpose spatial disjunction within the same frame as the laundrette is literally and figuratively split between the dancing heterosexual couple (Nasser and Rachel) in the foreground and the homosexual lovers in the background. But, contrary to the sequence that occurs earlier on in the film, the "laundrette sequence" negotiates a series of displacements within a lyricized space where the traumatized moments of private history are projected on to a wider social context; where "homely" moments are found within the "unhomely" and vice-versa, and the brutal world outside intrudes into the serene world inside. The twenty-three shots that constitute the "laundrette sequence" and its aftermath reveal the artificiality and conflicting juxtapositions of Kureishi/Frear's technique:

1. The camera focuses on the glitzy neon sign of the laundrette.
2. Title music comes on as the camera dissolves to a close-up shot of pretty colored fish swimming in a fish tank.
3. The music changes to a soft lyrical note as the camera pans across the painted walls of the laundrette with its blue and white clouds. The atmosphere inside is serene, pristine and dreamlike.
4. Medium shot of Omar and Johnny through the back room window.
5. They enter the back room. The room is bathed in soft blue and other warm colors as there is a slow shot reverse shot sequence between Johnny and Omar as they talk. Omar remembers the days when Johnny was a member of the right wing, anti-immigrant group with some bitterness.
6. Johnny is full of tenderness and remorse as he comes closer to Omar and begins to caress him as the camera closes up on them.
7. Cut to another close up of Johnny and Omar.
8. Cut to Rachel and Nasser as they enter the laundrette and look around. The camera zooms in on them as lyrical music begins to play.
9. Cut to the Johnny and Omar making love.
10. Cut to the dancing couple.
11. Cut to the couple making love.
12. Scenographic depth is created as the camera tilts backwards and enlarges the frame. Now we see both couples simultaneously as the screen splits between the heterosexual couple in the foreground and the homosexual couple in the background.
13. Close up of Rachel kissing Nasser.
14. Cut to the split screen. Nasser wonders where the two boys are and decides to marry Omar off.
15. Cut to Omar kissing Johnny.[34]
16. Camera follows Nasser as he walks towards the back door and walks in on Johnny and Omar dressing themselves. They walk out to the front of the laundrette.
17. Rachel inaugurates the opening of the laundrette by cutting the ribbon as Omar watches Johnny through the back window.
18. The doors of the laundrette open and people walk in with their laundry baskets.

19. Series of quick point of view shots as Rachel talks to Johnny and Omar talks to Nasser. Salim stands by the door watching.
20. Point of view shot as Johnny notices Tania at the door, holding a bouquet of flowers.
21. Quick point-of-view shots between Nasser, Tania, Omar and Rachel as they exchange nervous glances.
22. Camera tracks Johnny as he walks up to Tania and leads her towards Rachel. This is followed by a series of close-ups as Tania confronts Rachel. Nasser looks on uncomfortably.
23. Nasser leads Rachel out and we see them argue as the camera zooms out and there is a long shot of the two solitary lovers as they quarrel. They appear diminished against the glittering lights and tall buildings of London. Omar and Johnny's music is heard (ironically) in the background as they walk away from each other.

The pace of the camera movement quickens and the length of the shots shorten towards the end of the film as Nasser goes over to his brother's house and they begin to talk about themselves and their "homes". Interspersed between shots of Nasser and Hussein are sequences of violence as Genghis and his friends smash Salim's car and beat him. Johnny joins in and fights with his mates as Omar and Zaki walk back to "Powders". The screen once again assumes the tone, light, and texture of the earlier "realism" as Omar breaks up the fight and picks Johnny up and leads him to the back room in the laundrette and the film closes as the two lovers playfully splash water at each other. In the midst of "unhomely" turmoil and racial violence outside, another world becomes visible. And, in the intimate recesses of Omar's and Johnny's privatized union, the public and private conflate forcing us to recognize that within transgression lies belonging. In *My Beautiful Laundrette* love triumphs and ambition prevails. With Kureishi's second film, *Sammy and Rosie Get Laid*, the question of love and belonging are more complicated and the allegory is not easily accessible. Spivak writes:

> . . . the film juxtaposes a whole range of fact- finding, social engineering activities . . . the film gives us another spectrum of the social text . . . in each case you don't have just the one thing. You have a whole chain of displacements in terms of which you are shown how a quick fix or quick judgement or a quick read is productively resisted by the film.[35]

The elusiveness of Kureishi's second film, its aporetic quality, involves a significant and more overt move away from realism. In a certain sense the stylistic transformations and subtexts within the film give us a wide and conflicting spectrum of social life in contemporary Britain that *My Beautiful Laundrette* does not and the film's radicalism lies precisely in the deliberate misreadings it produces as a result of this. Thus, the movement from *My Beautiful Laundrette* to *Sammy and Rosie Get Laid* is a movement from private/public dichotomies to more collective identities. For Kureishi's second film continuously reminds us of the ubiquitous presence of other stories and histories. Unlike *My Beautiful Laundrette* where the evocation of the beauty of gay lovemaking is seen as a solution to the problems of racial difference, *Sammy and Rosie Get Laid* presents pleasure as a grotesque celebration that masks a sterile world of social, political, and economic repression. In *Sammy and Rosie* the codes of heterosexual love are mocked and political inconsistency is privileged as the characters release themselves from boundaries of imposed sexual, social, and political roles. The film consists of a bricolage of characters and concepts that are juxtaposed in a symbolic ensemble where original and straight meanings are constantly erased, threatened, or subverted. *Sammy and Rosie* attempts to "represent" the complex, multifaceted aesthetic and political meanings of diaspora culture. However, the focused difference in this film is not so much between postcolonial and migrant (although this is dealt with in the relation between Rafi and his son Sammy), but between different positions of radicalism as they interact with different aspects of postcoloniality and migrancy. By this I mean that Kureishi's second film etches cognitive and polyvocal spaces where social and hierarchical boundaries are momentarily suspended and replaced by a multiplicity of subject positions that signify what Gramsci might refer to as an **"organic crisis"**[36] whereby the emergence of new social forces no longer signify a coherent social order. What *Sammy and Rosie* does is activate the multi accentual quality of the sign which is, as Volosinov and Bakhtin point out ". . . is a very crucial aspect (of "class" struggle) . . . (as) each ideological sign has two faces, like Janus. This inner dialectic quality of the sign comes out fully into the open only in times of social crisis or revolutionary changes" (*Marxism*, 19). To the extent that Kureishi's film re-echoes Volosinov/Bakhtin's insight that the fixed meanings of signs become increasingly unstable, especially at moments of intense national/cultural struggle, it implies that the experimentation with certain kinds of unconventional techniques and subject matter can be a form of political intervention or cinema's attempt to decolonize dominant aesthetic practices. I believe *Sammy and Rosie* attempts to do this by enacting and embodying the spirit of **Carnival**.

The notion of "carnivalization" was first mentioned by Bakhtin in *Problems of Dostoyevsky's Poetics* where he elaborates his ideas concerning the transposition of the spirit of the carnival into art. However, it was not until *Rabelais and His*

Work that the notion was given its fullest formulation and it was not until Robert Stam published his *Subversive Pleasures: Bakhtin, Cultural Criticism and Film* that Bakhtin's concept was applied to filmic practice. In his book Stam explores the relevance of Bakhtin's carnivalesque to film and literature by drawing on its subversive potential.

In my reading of *Sammy and Rosie Get Laid*, I draw on Stam's notion of the carnivalesque spirit and associate it with the film's obsessive use of parody and grotesque realism. For Kureishi's film fetishizes inversions of power and displays an affinity with different forms of alterity. Its celebration of the forbidden, and the repressed represents a comic, almost joyful descent into contradiction, and, disagreeing with bell hooks, I must point out that the most ludicrous and comic moments of the film are also its most ironic and subversive moments.[37]
In this film masquerade functions to demystify and is embodied in the film's anarchic spirit—the spirit of the carnival which generates a heteroglossia of sexual, economic, social, and national differences. The discourse of carnival is also a counter discourse. Marked by oxymoronic characters, multiple and contradictory point of view, and styles, violations of every kind of social norm, the spirit of carnival in *Sammy and Rosie* ultimately challenges and defies our norms of decorum. Like *Handsworth Songs* (John Akomfrah, 1986) and *Territories* (Isaac Julien, 1984), Kureishi's film belongs to a group of black independent films in Britain that occupy a very specific space—a space where multiple configurations of races, histories, identities, sexualities create a dialogue between aspects of film language and aesthetics. Like *Handsworth Songs* and *Territories, Sammy and Rosie* also emphasizes it own performative mode of address. And, by destabilizing fixed modes of authority, it transgresses boundaries both at the level of aesthetics and subject matter. In this sense it embodies all the characteristics of the Notting Hill carnival that its predecessors did—the subversive nature of carnival, its ability to direct social change and challenge authority, and its ability to be more than a ritualized form of pleasure. *Sammy and Rosie,* then, rips off the mask of its own superficially festive and irresponsible surface to reveal deep fissures within contemporary British society.[38] Kureishi's film uses modes of irreverent pleasure to militate against official power and ideology—when the riots break out in the film. For example, Sammy smokes coke and listens to Shostakovich and Rosie accuses him of total disregard for what is happening outside. In fact, for all their political pretensions, none of the characters take any significant action during the riots. Anna hops around taking pictures of burning streets to add to her exhibition on scenes from a decaying Europe. Rosie speaks of the mass outside as the "affirmation of the human spirit," Sammy declares that "Leonardo da Vinci would

have lived in the inner city" and Danny/Victoria talks about the appropriateness of non-violence, Gandhi and Martin Luther King.

However, despite their seeming irreverence the riot scenes in *Sammy and Rosie* do represent a serious critique of mainstream, documentary rendering of racial violence that characterized the British media. Kureishi writes in his diary:

> ... we talk of avoiding the TV news footage approach: screaming mobs, bleeding policemen. What you don't get in news footage is detail. In *Battle of Algiers* the director humanizes violence. You see the faces of those whom the violence is being done ... [39]

In *Sammy and Rosie* we are shown a *different* version of the circumstance that gives rise to the violence on the streets. Using real life examples of Notting Hill, Brixton, and the Broadwater Farm uprisings, Kureishi gives us an insight into police instigated racial riots. But *Sammy and Rosie* is not about these riots as much as it presents the irony and problems of attempting to represent racial discord.[40] By using the carnivalesque mode by conflating rebellion and resistance through pleasure and revelry, Kureishi places the serious problem of racial violence in *Sammy and Rosie* squarely within the framework of Thatcher and her government's project to "clean up" the inner cities.

REPRESENTING MARGINALITY: THEORY, MASQUERADE AND "ORGANIC CRISIS" IN *SAMMY AND ROSIE GET LAID:*

I would like to propose a link between "home" and the Gramscian notion of organic **crisis** in *Sammy and Rosie Get Laid*, for Kureishi's second film raises a series of fundamental doubts about the homogeneity which was originally ascribed to English culture and society. For example, with the emergence of new social forces and the multiplicity of positions within the traditional British Left, it is almost impossible today to talk about a coherent English working class. Clearly, this has posed a serious problem for western Marxist cultural theorists who are now faced with a theoretical crisis because traditional notions of class difference and social change are no longer able to account for the rise of new subject positions, particularly the emergence of minority and subaltern cultures. Kureishi's film has been able to escape the totalizing tendencies of dominant Marxist theories by foregrounding the problems associated with transcendental theorizing. It does this by reconstructing these existing theories and by engaging in the historico-political process of constituting subjectivity without falling into the trap of easy generalizations.

Kureishi's London, then, evinces an 'organic crisis' where its inhabitants can no longer identify with a coherent notion of class, gender, and politics. Home for these people is merely a matter of intransigence where the characters continually (mis) read and (mis) represent each other. Take the case of Rafi and his daughter-in-law, Rosie. If in the words of Gayatri Chakravorty Spivak, Rosie represents "the indeterminate ideological subject of radicalism;" while Rafi represents the contradictory postcolonial elite; to grasp the complexity of their relationship we must look at the restaurant scene where the idealistic but slightly misguided Rosie confronts Rafi and accuses him of heinous crimes against his own people.

The activity of (mis) reading seems to be the modus operandi of this crucial scene where masquerade operates at two levels: at the level of language, particularly Kureishi/Frears' use of exaggeration and montage, and through the characters' sheer inability to read each other.

I read Kureishi/Frears' montage as *"intellectual montage"*—or an act of interpreting reality whereby film narration or technique is motivated by a highly tense emotional confrontation where we have to work through the non-coincident components of the film's narration. Montage's reliance on cutting in this particular segment of Kureishi/Frear's film provides a constant and ubiquitous rhetorical intervention where even the simple gestures are broken into several shots and the crosscutting provides the scene with a performative and highly charged quality. The atmosphere in the restaurant attains a surreal and dramatic quality with close-up shots of the screaming Rosie with her painted nails and weapon- like earrings; and the nonchalant Rafi eating a piece of human finger while the three women musicians play their violins with a deafening gusto:

1. The camera closes in on Rafi and Rosie as they eat their food and talk. Rosie asks Sammy to return his father's check. Sammy refuses, and the three continue to drink their wine and eat their dinner. Point-of-view shot of Rosie admiring a woman while Rafi looks on disapprovingly:
   ROSIE: That woman is a real star.
   RAFI: Now you're talking like a damn dyke.
2. Medium shot of the three characters—a frontal shot of Rosie as she begins to accuse Rafi—and profile shots of Rafi and Sammy.
3. The camera frame is enlarged to include the three women musicians playing the violin, all of them bearing an uncanny resemblance to the portrait of Virginia Woolf in Rosie's room.
4. The camera cuts back and forth between Rafi and Rosie as they argue. Close up of Rafi as he bites a piece of human finger and Rosie looks on.

5. The pace of the camera movement increases as the pitch of Rosie's voice increases. Rafi asks for more wine.

6. A series of quick, short shots between Rafi and Rosie as the musicians strum ferociously on their violins. This is followed by two quick close-ups of the violinists as they desperately try to drown the voices of Rafi and Rosie. The waiter interrupts, the woman Rosie admired throws her napkin and walks out in a huff, and Sammy looks on and tries to control the spectacle.

7. Final shot of Rafi and Rosie as the camera freezes on their profiles and Rafi delivers his soliloquy on nationalism, patriotism, and colonialism.

In this sequence, the political efficacy of montage lies clearly in its ability to fragment points of view and expose disparities; to shatter the homogeneity of spectacle. Thus, Rafi nonchalantly eats the human finger as Rosie accuses him of torture and every bit of Rosie's "simple-minded" ethics is undercut by close ups of her shouting at Rafi like a caged vulture about to tear into her prey. The violence associated with Rosie's close ups, her dress, her exaggerated make-up and jewelry undermine Rafi's tranquility when he discusses imperialism and violence.

One other aspect of the restaurant scene deserves to be commented on; Kureishi's outrageous and flamboyant manipulation of montage to draw analogies and reinforce links between "unlike" things where the narration will "flash back" echoes of earlier scenes. For instance, Kureishi/Frear's intercutting of Rafi and Rosie's argument with shots of the three women violinists, one of who resembles the burning portrait of Virginia Woolf in Rosie's study, and Rafi's obvious disapproval of Rosie's admiration of the woman in the restaurant, remind us of previous scenes when Rafi, outraged by Vivia and Rani's transgressive sexuality, is constantly haunted by the possibility that his daughter-in-law might be a lesbian! Here Kureishi/Frears spectacalize Rafi's prudery and uncertainty by reusing an image from the past (the burning portrait of Virginia Woolf as it appears in Rafi's dream) in a different way by transferring it on to a different context (the woman violinist in the restaurant). Here, the spectator must take the visual cues to draw analogies because, clearly, in this case, conceptual parallelism replaces causal logic to wedge an ironic relationship between sexuality and politics. Rafi clearly (mis) reads this relationship:

> RAFI: You are only concerned with homosexuals and women! A luxury that rich oppressors can afford! We were concerned with poverty, imperialism, feudalism! Real issues . . .[41]

"Montage" as it operates in the "restaurant scene" uses the ironic interplay of character and dialogue to "produce . . . some effects of work":

> . . . it multiplies traces, cuts, gaps, fractures, in short the signs of writing (ecriture) which affirm it as being an operation by which, again at the very least, it shows that there is a work of signifying production: it watches itself . . . Reworking the status of the images in the signifying network, redistributing their positions, reorganizing their relations according to systems of opposition or recurrence, dividing and denaturalizing their mechanical linkup, montage superimposes upon that flowing emergence of an impression of reality, which every series of images (edited or not) necessarily produces, another movement, that of meaning of reading.[42]

So, when Rosie accuses Rafi of torture and fascist crimes, she misreads him and his history and Rafi responds in a defensive but matter of fact way:

> RAFI: You are only concerned with homosexuals and women! A luxury that rich oppressors can afford! We are concerned with poverty, imperialism, feudalism! Real issues that burn people! . . . A man who hasn't killed is a virgin and doesn't understand the word love! The man who sacrifices others to the benefit of the whole is in a terrible position. But he is essential! Even you know that. I come from a land ground in dust by two hundred years of imperialism. We are still dominated by the west and you reproach us for the methods you taught us. I helped people for their own good and damaged others for the same reason just like you in your feeble profession![43]

In India, bourgeois opposition to imperialism was always ambiguous. Paradoxically, after independence, the national government in its dealings with the local masses is reminiscent of certain features of the former colonial powers. So Rafi, once a committed freedom fighter, becomes a bourgeois businessman and re-enacts a different form of imperialism in his own country. The violence by which colonial structures were imposed now became an integral part of Rafi's (post) colonial psyche—his internal "organic crisis" which ultimately leads him to break ties with his own homeland and histories, to become the displaced, postmodern, postcolonial bourgeois—unmasked, haunted, unscrupulous, cynical, with nowhere to go. Conditioned by the antagonisms of colonial society, Rafi is alienated from himself and represents the central contradiction that nationalism in India/Pakistan experienced. Setting out to assert his freedom from British colonialism, he remains prisoner of western discourse and ethics. But Rosie's political discourse and bourgeois background cannot account for the multiplicity and complexities of Rafi's position(s) as committed freedom fighter, national bourgeois oppressor, and dispossessed postcolonial.

The simplicity of Rosie's accusations represents a wider crisis in classical Marxist theories that posit oppression solely within the general framework of working class oppression. Gayatri Spivak writes that Rosie's position is ". . . the beleaguered position of the civilized conscience for whom torture is bad under any circumstance . . . And the reason that one can't read Rosie is that she dramatizes the confrontation between radicalism and an old-fashioned simple morality based on a rather simple ethics" (*Outside*, 247–248).

As a matter of fact, all the characters in *Sammy and Rosie* are figures of discursive unease because they never are what they appear to be. Nor do they relate or understand each other in any substantial way. They are complicated, even though they resemble cardboard caricatures of particular "types". They also resist stereotypical reductions based on race, gender, political, and economic status. Take the case of Danny/Victoria in the film. Victoria's belief in "passive revolution" invokes both the nationalistic tradition of Gandhi (Britain's colonial connection) as well as Martin Luther King. Yet it combines with it the respectable and very English tradition vaguely reminiscent of William Goodwin. Raymond Williams describes Goodwin and his circle in his essay **"The Bloomsbury Fraction"**:

> . . . Goodwin and his friends were relatively poor working professionals, an emerging small-bourgeoisie, with no other means of social or political influence. In their basic attempt to establish rationality, tolerance, and liberty they were opposing . . . a whole class and system beyond them. Within their own group they could argue for and try to practice the rational values of civilized equality . . . including sexual equality . . . The rational and civilizing proposals were not with the crudest kind of repression, prosecution, imprisonment, and transportation . . . It is a remarkable moment in English culture . . . [44]

Thus, even though Goodwin's group was a failure, Williams recognized it as culturally significant if only for the nobility of its aspirations and the inherent character of its illusions.

Victoria's connection to Goodwin's group is clearly his pacifism, which represents a celebration of rebelliousness that characterized young anarchist groups in Britain. In many ways the character of Victoria was also conceptualized through the idealism of some of the young people in Kureishi's own theater workshops. Kureishi writes in his diary:

. . . they had terrific energy, intelligence and inventiveness, unemployment and bad schooling, they were living in the interstices of society; studying in squats, dealing drugs and generally scavenging around. It seemed . . . society had little to offer them, no idea how to use them or what to do with their potential.[45]

It seems to me that the character of Danny was conceptualized out of the variety of discourses that in turn spur several different (mis) readings and Victoria himself is not an exception to this. He, in turn, (mis) reads; by confusing India with Pakistan. Danny tells Rafi: ". . . after all, your way is just to sit down and be non-violent and that's what we really ought to learn."[46] And, of course, Rafi agrees wholeheartedly and takes on the position of the patriotic postcolonial in a way that strikes one as oddly ironic when one recalls both Rafi's earlier defense of torture and Danny's justification of the violent riots that erupt after the shooting of the black woman.

But these are positive (mis) readings because, as Spivak points out, great mobilizing signifiers of political action emerge from these sorts of misreadings. The viewer is never able to grasp the 'essential' nature of either Rafi's postcoloniality or Danny's brand of non-violent anarchism (as if the two are even compatible) and the distance between reading and representation is further initiated by the 'unreality' or surreality of Victoria as the idealized angelic avenger.

The problem of fixing meaning and finding a common language/history is continuously explored as part of the film's "organic crisis" and the plurality of subjectivities that exist. For instance, the single group of people that meets at Sammy and Rosie's house indicates that the social and cultural significance of groups like that lies precisely in their inability to adhere to any fixed set of formulations. Rosie is a left-wing writer and social worker whose sympathies clearly lie with the downtrodden. A free spirit, she clearly enjoys sleeping with men from the fringes of society. Danny/Victoria appreciatively describes her as deliberately downwardly mobile. Anna, Sammy's girlfriend represents the uninhibited New York photographer. Typical of her class and background, her goal is to spectacalize violence and poverty for mass consumption. Alice, Rafi's lady friend represents all that is sacred and respectable in British middle class urban society. Her connection with Rosie's group is her colonial connection. She grew up in India and spent her whole life waiting for Rafi to come back to her. Unable to understand Vivia's enjoyment of "pure" pleasure; she is nonetheless fascinated with the idea of sexual gratification for women. Rani (Asian) and Vivia (black) are "politically committed" lesbians who are engaged in a "fact finding" mission, hoping to track down Rafi's involvement with his government's reactionary regime. Gayatri Spivak comments on their "control of the entire spectrum of language use":

> They move from an expository fact-finding use of English, in the scene in the office where the woman who speaks with a fairly heavy accent is Chinese-British, to hurling abuse in Urdu. This is boldly different from modeling gay male love on straight romance . . . [47]

This is entirely true because although Vivia and Rani are kept well outside the realm of the uninhibited pleasure of the copulating couples in the "fuck scene"; theirs is the only desire that is truly articulated in terms of political praxis. Unable to understand Rosie's heterosexual, middle class, values, both Vivia and Rani are constantly set against the grain in Kureishi's film. Their transgressive sexuality is used (and sometimes spectacalized) as a foil against Rafi's prudery and reactionary, patriarchal politics, or against the sterile, heterosexual relationship between Rosie and Sammy. It is also used to undermine Asian taboos against homosexuality, particularly the characterization of it as a purely western phenomenon.

The intermingling of races, classes, and political and sexual inclinations in *Sammy and Rosie* constantly reminds us, as Spivak points out, that "on the other side of white is a variety of blackness." The plurality of positions articulated in Kureishi's film indicate a rupture or crisis within English society that was once considered to be homogenous. Vivia and Rani are unable to understand Rosie's brand of socialism and when Rosie does not allow them to confront Rafi with his political actions, they accuse her of being a "liberal" with a surface politics typical of her middle class background. Thus, the infiltration of affluent middle-class subjects (like Rosie) along with the emergence of different and multiple races (Sammy, Vivia, Rani, Danny) into the previously unified British classes, disrupted the traditional definition of class and empire. As a result, any expectations of "belonging" seem increasingly inadequate. According to Kenneth Kaleta, "Rafi succinctly transfers the film's surreal juxtaposition of visual and political messages into literal message when he puts the urban riots into words, on a postcard he sends back to Pakistan: 'Streets on fire—wish you were here'" (*Hanif*, 53–54). In fact, the only scene in the entire film that remotely indicates a sense of belonging, is Sammy's "London sequence." Rafi points out to Sammy that, for him, London no longer represented "hot buttered toast on a fork in front of the open fire", but of another version of Beirut—"a cesspit" which could never be "home" for Sammy.

Sammy responds by asserting that London is truly home in a sequence where he describes the different aspects of the city that he loves and enjoys. This is the only sequence where the city is lyricized, even romanticized in the film. Here, we are taken through several London scenes that Sammy and Rosie enjoy, like walking towards Hammersmith Bridge, or browsing through bookstores, or going to the Royal Court Theater or alternative cabaret at Earl's Court or attending Colin MaCabe's lecture on Derrida , Lacan, and semiotics at the ICA or Institute of Contemporary Art. Sammy ends his soliloquy by declaring that: "We love our city and belong to it. Neither of us are English, we're Londoners you see." And this difference between being English and being a Londoner is crucial for Sammy's diasporic sense of "belonging", and this Rafi, as a postcolonial elite cannot understand. Clearly Sammy cannot escape the "organic crisis" that characterized a severely divided nation; but he can and is able to find a niche for himself in a city that is clearly able to provide a space for his uprooted identity and migrant sensibility. Despite the displacements that characterize Sammy's walk through London where "hostilities are provisionally suspended" by London's fluidity and endless possibilities, Sammy's fascination with the city allows him to fabricate a sense of belonging.

CARNIVAL, MASQUERADE, AND THE POLITICS OF PLEASURE:

Carnivalesque or masquerading strategies in *Sammy and Rosie Get Laid* aim to unmask or demystify the contradictions masked by sanguine reality by constantly reminding us of the existence of other stories, traditions, histories and pleasures. If we look at the central "fuck scene" in Kureishi's film we notice an eroticized blurring of political and social boundaries where questions of race, class, and color are uninhibitedly and promiscuously leveled and commingled. This segment is also an example of the film's interesting use of montage. Linking bodily pleasure to larger sociopolitical issues, Kureishi/Frears emphasize the notion of pleasure given to excess and radical differentiality where middle-class prudery is mocked and political and sexual inconsistency privileged. Kenneth Kaleta describes this as one of the most "inventive" sequences in *Sammy and Rosie* (*Hanif,* 56). The *New York Times* reviewed the scene as follows:

> About three quarters of the way through *Sammy and Rosie Get Laid,* there's a particularly rich, riotously busy montage, a succession of shots of urban decay, exuberant West Indian street singers and three separate shots of lovers who alternately reminisce and argue while, at the end of a long London night, they make their circuitous routes to bed. The tempo of the editing increases. Suddenly,

the screen splits-horizontally-and we see each of the three couples, layered, more or less, one pair atop another, simultaneously but in separate images, as they achieve transitory satisfaction. That's about all they can hope for.[48]

The split screen of the "fuck scene" does not allow us to view the sexual act purely in terms of pleasure, even though the copulating couples are unified by the singular act of sex. This is because, here, the political, racial, and social differences, although they masquerade as "pure" pleasure, are attempts to recoup in sexual fantasy what is prohibited in reality. In a sense, this collective *jouissance* is ironic because it conveys a false sense of unity and fulfillment. In fact, I believe, what the split scene emphasizes, is exactly the opposite. By parodying conventional norms of romantic lovemaking, here, pleasure is seen as a grotesque celebration that masks a world of disjunctions—a sterile world of political, social, and economic repression.

Yet, the "fuck scene" operates at two levels. It is both an erotic violation of norms as well as a critique of pure pleasure precisely because it uses masquerade to deploy the force of dominant culture against itself. For Kureishi, pleasure can only exist in relation to something else.

In his submerged polemic with pleasure, Kureishi highlights the constructed nature of its discourse, always short circuiting its titillating value of image and language to make the spectator conscious of her/his investment in cinematic voyerism (the scene between Vivia and Rani dangling a carrot is another example of this). Thus, in *Sammy and Rosie*, although sex masquerades as pleasure and transgression and is not intrinsically subversive, it is always important to ask who is having sex with whom and for what reasons and under what circumstances? The lust, crudity, and clumsiness that characterizes Rafi's lovemaking with Alice, or the bohemian lovemaking of Anna and Sammy, or the overtly uninhibited and romantic lovemaking of Danny and Rosie are all juxtaposed in a single frame to signal dissonant aspects of pleasure. Here, pleasure no longer possesses a universal language. In fact, the entire sequence of events and shots that lead up to the climactic split screen montage invoke the presence of dissonance. At the level of technique, the jarring decoupage and quick intercutting of short scenes that lead up to the sequence, contrast with the soft, sensuous, warm colors that shroud the dream-like, surreal, glowing, carnivalesque, mise-en-scene of Danny's commune where the straggly band dressed in colorful drag serenade outside Danny's caravan with the lyrics of "My Girl". Juxtaposed with Rafi's relatively sterile lovemaking in Alice's suburban home, and the dangerously exhilarating roof of Anna's studio where Anna and Sammy make love, the scene in Danny's caravan appears ironically romantic, and idealized.

The film's tempo changes in the scenes that follow the "fuck scene". Now the segments are shorter, edited by quick enjambments as Rafi is rejected by Alice and everyone else in his family. Eventually he seeks refuge in Danny's commune where he confronts the unpleasant ghosts of his past.

The layers of discourse invoked by the ghost in *Sammy and Rosie* is another example of Kureishi/Frear's use of montage—particularly the scene in Alice's basement where a very English literary tradition is echoed and recast within a framework of black film counter discourse.[49] The scene is important because it signals a complicated relationship between postcoloniality, gender, nation, and empire. The presence of the "invisible" ghost figure that signifies history and memory adds further complexity to the scene. Thus, in this basement scene, montage functions as an act of interpreting reality, whereby Kureishi/Frears do not simply represent reality but ask us to (re) construct it.

Masquerading first as the Pakistani cab driver that drives Rafi from the airport, the ghost haunts Rafi by following him wherever he goes. Reappearing in Alice's basement and Danny's caravan, it embodies Rafi's problematic relation to history because it is the central figure through which Kureishi combines, collides and (mis) represents Indian, Pakistani, and British history. Dressed up in a miner's helmet with a smashed head and blind eye, he parodies a plurality of histories and reminds us of the copresence of multiple stories[50]—the coal miner's strike in England, the Bhagalpur blindings of Emergency India, atrocities of both colonial and postcolonial regimes that remind Rafi of his own involvements in the propagation of terror and torture. The ghost reminds us that history is not always linear. It can be ambiguous and facts are hard to establish because they can mean different things simultaneously. Reading the ghost's "unreliability" into the narration of Kureishi's film, then, is a useful analogy of the way every character in the film attempts to (mis) read the other. Kureishi's ghost conflates and turns the political and postcolonial problems of violence and the need for an uncontaminated and complete sense of belonging full circle where the postcolonial is ultimately not able to escape the despair of his own legacy of aggression. In the end Rafi has no choice but to seek refuge in death—his limits are unmasked by the ghost—"who locates the sins of both indigenous capital and crimes against the labor unions",[51] of colonial aggression and postcolonial terror—of "history as an open wound" (*Outside*, 254), and of belonging as contingent.

Figure 1. Hanif Kureishi, *My Beautiful Laundrette*

Figure 2. Hanif Kureishi, *Sammy and Rosie Get Laid*

NOTES

1. Mikhail Bakhtin, *The Dialogic Imagination,* trans. Carl Emerson and Michael Holquist (Austin: U of Texas P, 1981) 163.

2. Teshome Gabriel, "Thoughts on Nomadic Aesthetics and the Black Independent Cinema: Traces of a Journey," *Blackframes: Critical Perspectives in Black Independent Cinema,* eds. M. Cham and C. Andrade-Watkins (Cambridge, MIT P, 1988) 72.

3. Salman Rushdie, *Imaginary Homelands* (London: penguin, 1991) 10.

4. Gayatri Chakravorty Spivak, "In Praise of *Sammy and Rosie Get Laid,*" *Critical Quarterly* 31.2 (1989): 80.

5. See Dick Hebdige, *Subculture: The Meaning of Style* (London: Routledge, 1979). Hebdige's book focuses on the emergence of youth subcultures in Britain. However, Hebdige does analyze in some depth the relations between white youth subcultures like the skinheads and their explosive relations with black (particularly Pakistani) immigrants. He writes ". . . patterns of rejection and assimilation between host and immigrant communities can be mapped along the spectacular lines laid down by the white working-class youth cultures. The succession of white subcultural forms can be read as a series of deep-structural adaptations which symbolically accommodate or expunge the black presence from the host community" (44). However, Hebdige observes this dialogue between the two cultures takes the form of a "frozen dialectic". ". . . a dialectic which beyond a point (i.e.) ethnicity is incapable of renewal, trapped as it is within its own history, imprisoned within its own irreducible antinomies" (70).

6. M.M. Bakhtin, "The Problems of Speech Genres", *Speech Genres and Other Late Essays,* trans. Vern McGee (Austin: U of Texas P, 1986) 91.

7. See Robert Stam, *Subversive Pleasures: Bakhtin, Cultural Criticism, and Film* (Baltimore: Johns Hopkins, 1989), Kobena Mercer, "Diaspora Culture and the Dialogic Imagination: The Aesthetics of Black Independent Film in Britain," *Blackframes: Critical Perspectives on Black Independent Cinema,* eds. M.Cham and C. Andrade-Watkins (Cambridge: MIT P, 1988).

8. Robert Stam, *Subversive Pleasures: Bakhtin, Cultural Criticism, and Film* (Baltimore: Johns Hopkins, 1989) 187–218.

9. Robert Stam, *Subversive Pleasures:Bakhtin, Cultural Criticism, and Film* (Baltimore: Johns Hopkins, 1989) 191–192.

10. I borrow this term from Salman Rushdie. See Salman Rushdie, *Imaginary Homelands* (London: Penguin, 1991).

11. See Teshome Gabriel, "Thoughts on Nomadic Aesthetics and the Black Independent Cinema: Traces of a Journey" *Blackframes: Critical Perspectives on Black Independent Cinema,* eds. M. Cham and C. Andrade-Watkins (Cambridge: MIT P, 1988) 73–74. Here

Gabriel discusses the notion of the mask as screen where he views the screen like a mask that restructures one's viewing habits by both deframing the world and disguising meaning.

12. For more information on how definitions of home, community and exile have shifted and are represented in the media within the new global context, see Hamid Naficy, ed. *Home, Exile, Homeland: Film, Media, And the Politics of Place* (New York and London" Routledge, 1999).

13. Hanif Kureishi, *London Kills Me* (New York: Penguin, 1992) 100–101.

14. Cary Nelson and Lawrence Grossberg, eds. *Marxism and the Interpretation of Culture* (Chicago: University of Illinois P, 1988) 53.

15. Stuart Hall and Tony Jefferson, eds. *Resistance Through Rituals: Youth Subcultures in Post-War Britain* (London: Harper Collins Academic, 1976) 100–102.

16. Thatcherism was radically different from older versions of conservatism because it combined the different elements of conservatism in a distinct and original way. The most novel aspect of Thatcherism, Stuart Hall points out, was the way in which it *combined* the new doctrines of free market with the older values and traditions of Englishness, patriarchalism, family, nation, respectability etc. On matters of policy, this meant reversing state subsidies, welfare, cutting back on public spending and restoring free market forces, underpinning profitability and breaking the power of the working class and trade unions creating a further decline in the living standard of both white sub-classes and their immigrant counterparts. However, many immigrants of Indian and Pakistani origin began to adopt the styles and mannerisms of the dominant classes by grabbing the opportunities provided to them by Thatcher's free enterprise policies. Thus, they adopted a work ethic and way of life that was very different from their white working class counterparts and while they continued to cling to their traditions and customs they began to assimilate with the dominant classes by starting small businesses and engaging in any sort of profitable enterprise. See Stuart Hall, "The Toad in the Garden: Thatcherism among the Theorists," *Marxism and the Interpretation of Culture*, eds. Cary Nelson and Lawrence Grossberg, (Chicago: U of Illinois P, 1988), Dilip Hiro, *Black British, White British*, (London:Paladin, 1992), Stuart Hall and Tony Jefferson, eds., *Resistance Through Rituals: Youth Subcultures in Post-War Britain*, (London: Harper Collins Academic, 1976).

17. Hanif Kureishi, *London Kills Me* (New York: Penguin, 1992) 48.

18. Cary nelson and Lawrence Grossberg, eds. *Marxism and the Interpretation of Culture* (Chicago: U of Illinois P, 1988) 40–42.

19. Dick Hebdige, *Subculture: The Meaning of Style* (London: Routledge, 1991) 41–42.

20. Hanif Kureishi, *London Kills Me* (New York: Penguin, 1992) 73.

21. Hanif Kureishi, *London Kills Me* (New York: Penguin, 1992)50.

22. Hanif Kureishi, *London Kills Me* (New York: Penguin, 1992) 105.

23. Hanif Kureishi, *London Kills Me* (New York: Penguin, 1992) 106.

24. Gayatri Chakravorty Spivak, "In Praise of *Sammy and Rosie Get Laid*" *Critical Quarterly* 31.2 (1989): 82.

25. Hanif Kureishi, *London Kills Me* (New York: Penguin, 1992) 73.

26. Kobena Mercer uses the phrase "performative body politics" in his discussion of Marlon Riggs's film *Tongues United* in which the eroticized black bodies of gay men are sites of misery, oppression, exploitation and resistance. In my reading of Kureishi's film, however, "performative body politics" implies an enactment of eroticized gay bodies that affirm it not as a site of exploitation but that of resistance, transgression, and ecstasy. See Kobena Mercer, "Dark and Lovely Too: Black Gay Men in Independent Film," *Queer Looks: Perspectives on Lesbian and Gay Film and Video*, eds. Martha Gever, John Greyson, and Pratibha Parmar, (New York and London: Routledge, 1993) 247.

27. Kenneth Kaleta, *Hanif Kureishi: Postcolonial Storyteller*, (Austin: U of Texas P, 1998) 176–177.

28. Teshome Gabriel, "Thoughts on Nomadic Aesthetics and the Black Independent Cinema: Traces of a Journey," *Out There: Marginalization and Contemporary Culture*, eds. Russell Ferguson, et. Al. (Cambridge: MIT Press, 1990) 405.

29. Julian Henriques, "Realism and the New Language," *Black Film British Cinema,* Institute of Contemporary Art (London:BFI 1988) 19.

30. Julian Henriques, "Realism and the New language," *Black Film British Cinema*, Institute of Contemporary Art (London: BFI) 19.

31. Norman Stone, "Through a Lens Darkly," *Black Film British Cinema*, Institute of Contemporary Art (London: BFI, 1988) 22.

32. Julian Henriques, "Realism and the New Language," *Black Film British Cinema*, Institute of Contemporary Art (London: BFI, 1988) 19.

33. I borrow this term from Homi Bhabha who writes about "unhomely" moments as being paradigmatic post-colonial experiences where domestic spaces become sites of displacements. See Homi Bhabha, "The World and the Home," *Social Text* 31/32 (1992).

34. The dissonance between dialogue and image to create ironic effects characteristic of Kureishi/Frears' technique is apparent here. So, in this scene, while Nasser makes plans to marry Omar off, the camera cuts to a close up of Johnny and Omar making love or when Nasser talks to his brother Hussein about "home" and proclaims that compared to Pakistan, England is a "little heaven", the camera cuts to scenes of violence and racial discord between Salim and lads outside the laundrette. This technique is, however, more frequently used in Kureishi's second film, *Sammy and Rosie Get Laid*.

35. Gayatri Chakravorty Spivak, "In Praise of *Sammy and Rosie Get Laid*" *Critical Quarterly* 31.2 (1989): 87.

36. I borrow the term "**organic crisis**" from Antonio Gramsci. According to Gramsci, at a certain point in their historical lives, social classes become detached from their political parties. Gramsci writes: "In other words, the traditional parties in that particular organizational form, with the particular men who constitute, represent, and lead them, are no longer recognized by their class (or fraction of a class) as its expression" (210). However, Gramsci points out, when this crisis occurs, the immediate situation becomes "delicate and dangerous" because the masses are not capable of reorganizing with the same rhythm as the dominant classes. But the traditional ruling class, ". . . which has numerous trained cadres, changes men and programs and, with greater speed than is achieved by the subordinate classes, re-absorbs the control that was slipping from its grasp" (210). The swing to the right, then, is part of an 'organic' phenomenon. However, this swing is not a reflection of the crisis but a *response* to it. The term is later used by Stuart Hall in his critique and analysis of the appeal of Thatcherism in Great Britain. According to Stuart Hall, Thatcher built her popularity by creating a false sense of unity and consensus by creating a new form of popular will and by exploiting and capitalizing the moment of crisis that the Labor government was facing. Stuart Hall writes:"Ideologically, Thatcherism is seen as forging new discursive articulations between the liberal discourses of the "free market" and economic man and the organic conservative themes of tradition, family and nation, respectability, patriarchalism and order. Its reworking of these different repertoires of 'Englishness' constantly repositions both the individual subjects and 'the people' as a whole—their needs, experiences, aspirations, pleasure and desires . . ." (2). And it did this while the Labor government was not able to find a way to address the changing needs of its party. Characterized by the emergence of new social, sexual, and ethnic identities, the Labor left was not able to reconcile or create consensus between the different and multiple needs of its constituents. The left no longer constituted a homogenous working class. In fact the intrusion of the new, intellectualized middle class into the confines of the traditional left disrupted its homogeneity. Thatcher's victory, then, can partly be attributed to the Labor party's inability to deal with its "organic crisis" and this chaotic heterogeneity is clearly evident in *Sammy and Rosie*, particularly in the group that meets at Sammy's and Rosie's apartment. See Antonio Gramsci, *Selections from the Prison Notebooks*, (New York: International Publishers, 1991), Stuart Hall, *The Hard Road to Renewal: Thatcherism and the Crisis of the Left*, (London and New York: Verso, 1988).

37. See bell hooks, *Yearning: Race, Gender, and Cultural Politics* (Boston: South End Press, 1990). Hooks believes that the comic and farcical elements in the film are the reasons why the film cannot be read as subversive and serious. I believe that the comedy in Kureishi's film is both ironic and carnivalesque in that it displays an ability to be subversive by mocking bourgeois decorum. Comedy and pleasure in the film are grotesque celebrations that mask a sterile and repressive political, social, and economic world.

38. Much has been said about the relationship between the spirit of carnival and black independent counter-films. Notting Hill has become the central example of authoritarian repression and resistance through revelry and pleasure. When, in 1976, black youth actively resisted police attempts to close and contain the Notting Hill carnival, the role of the carnival, though not inherently subversive, came to represent a means by which resistance could be expressed. Thus, both *Territories* and *Handsworth Songs*, though not actively about Notting Hill, became examples of film's ability to subvert through the enactment of the critical spirit of the carnival. It is my belief that Kureishi's second film embodies this spirit and it is the "carnivalizing" codes of masquerade and montage that make the film subversive. For more information on "carnivalization" and film see M.Cham and C.Andrade-Watkins, eds. *Blackframes: Critical Perspectives on Black Independent Cinema* (Cambridge: MIT P, 1988) and Robert Stam's *Subversive Pleasures: Bakhtin, Cultural Criticism, and Film* (Baltimore: Johns Hopkins, 1989).

39. Hanif Kureishi, *Sammy and Rosie Get Laid* (New York: Penguin, 1988) 79.

40. He first scene in Kureishi's film is based on the actual shooting of a black woman (Cherry Groce) by an indifferent white policeman and once again, disagreeing with bell hooks, I must point out that the randomness of the shooting is *not* undermined by the shot of the woman flinging hot oil on the policeman because the shots that precede it clearly establish that the woman's action was motivated by self-defense. The policemen shout as they enter the building and the violinist (her son) hides in expectation of trouble giving sufficient warning to the woman that there is trouble round the corner. The dilemma of representing black violence has been discussed at length by several black independent filmmakers and I believe that by humanizing the violence in his film Kureishi is at least able to incorporate the point of view of the black victim. The fast paced riot sequences at the beginning of the film work in conjunction with the ritualistic departure of Danny's commune and the cleaning up of the "inner cities" at the end of the film. While these sequences provide the backdrop or framework of the film; they are also important examples of Kureishi's infusion of spectacle with violence to highlight the "constructedness" or "non-naturalness" of all discourse. By refusing to recognize the subversive potential of Kureishi's "carnivalizing" techniques, hooks has simply reduced Kureishi's polemics to "the comic". For Kureishi there are no neat little politically correct areas—only murky and shadowy spaces. See bell hooks *Yearning: Race, Gender, and Cultural Politics* (Boston: South End Press, 1990).

41. Hanif Kureishi, *London Kills Me* (New York: Penguin, 1992) 229.

42. David Bordwell, *Narration in the Fiction Film* (Madison: U of Wisconsin P, 1985) 271.

43. Hanif Kureishi, *London Kills Me* (New York: Penguin, 1992) 229.

44. Hanif Kureishi, *Sammy and Rosie Get Laid* (New York: Penguin, 1988) 157.

45. Hanif Kureishi, *Sammy and Rosie Get Laid* (New York: Penguin, 1988) 70.

46. Gayatri Chakravorty Spivak points out that Danny/Victoria's misreading of India echoes other misreadings, like Martin Luther King's misreading of Gandhi. See "In Praise of *Sammy and Rosie Get Laid*" *Critical Quarterly* 31.2 (1989).

47. Gayatri Chakravorty Spivak, *Outside in theTeaching Machine* (New York and London: Routledge, 1993) 249.

48. Vincent Canby, "Chaotic London" *New York Times* October, 30, 1987.

49. The scene recalls a Dickens novel. The spooky atmosphere of the basement where Alice opens her old, musty trunk and flings her clothes, letters, and memories at Rafi while she recalls how she spent all her life waiting for him, echoes the grotesque and gothic ambiance of *Great Expectations*. Alice's solitude and bitter and frenzied confrontation with Rafi reminds us of Miss Havisham's exaggerated response to her unhappy fate.

50. The multitudanal discourses invoked by the ghost are accentuated by Kureishi's use of music (Indipop), particularly in the scene that follows the "cellar scene" in Alice's house when Rafi walks through the streets of London followed by the ghost. While music is always below the threshold, subtle, never very loud, it is an extraordinary fusion of styles—blues, r 'n' b mixed with Hindi film songs, Punjabi bhangra music, African drumming, and traces of reggae!

51. Gayatri Chakravorty Spivak, *Outside in the Teaching Machine* (New York and London: Routledge, 1993) 254.

CHAPTER TWO

Beyond the Rushdie Affair: Women, Masquerade, and Translation in *The Satanic Verses*

It was Uma who pursued me through my dreams, dead Uma, made frightful by death, Uma wild-haired, white —eyed, fork tongued, Uma metamorphosed into an angel of revenge, playing a hellbat Dis-demona to my Moor. Fleeing from her I would run into a mighty fortress, slam its door shut, turn—and find myself outside once again, and she floating in air, above me and behind, Uma with Vampire's fangs the size of elephant's tusks. And again in front of me was a fortress, its doors standing open, offering me sanctuary; and again I ran, and slammed the door, and found myself still in the open air, defenseless, at her mercy. 'You know how the Moor built' she whispered to me. 'Theirs was mosaic architecture of interlinked insides and outsides . . . But you—I condemn you to exteriors from now on . . . Across these infinite outsides I will hunt you down.' Then she came down to me, and opened her awful mouth[1]

On the mantelpiece he keeps a small group of postcards bearing conventional images of his homeland, which he calls simply Desh . . . But in his bedroom, on the wall facing the hard cot where he lies, there hangs a more potent icon, the portrait of a woman of exceptional force, famous for her profile of a Grecian statue . . . A powerful woman, his enemy, his other: he keeps her close . . . She is the Empress, and her name is—what else? Ayesha. On this island, the exiled imam, and at home in Desh, She. They plot each other's death.[2]

In a post-colonial context the problematic of *translation* becomes a significant site for raising questions of representation, power and historicity. The contest is one of

contesting and contested stories attempting to account for, to recount, the
asymmetry and inequality of relations between peoples, races, languages . . . [3]

. . . What I had on my hands was an almost excessively masculine tale, a saga of
sexual rivalry, ambition, power, patronage, betrayal, death, revenge. But the
women seem to have taken over; they marched in from the peripheries of the story
to demand the inclusion of their own tragedies, histories, and comedies . . . to see
my "male" plot refracted, . . . through the prisms of its reverse "female" side. [4]

The post-colonial desire to *re-translate* is linked to the desire to re-write *history*.
Rewriting is based on an act of reading, for translation in the post- colonial context
involves what Benjamin would call "citation" and not "absolute forgetting." Hence
there is no simple rupture with the past but a radical rewriting of it. To read
existing translations against the grain is also to read colonial historiography from a
post-colonial perspective, and a critic alert to the ruses of colonial discourse can
help uncover what Walter Benjamin calls "the second tradition," the history of
resistance. This act of *remembering, as* Bhabha has pointed out, "is never a quiet
act of introspection or retrospection." Rather, it is "a painful re-membering, a
putting together of the dismembered past to make sense of the trauma of the
present. [5]

If the nation is an imagined community, that imagining is profoundly gendered . . .
National fantasies, be they colonial, anti-colonial or post-colonial, also play upon
and with the connections between women, land or nations. [6]

In the autumn of 1988 a debate started in Great Britain. It concerned Salman
Rushdie's novel *The Satanic Verses.* Never has a debate about a work of literature
had such a far-flung effect on intellectuals, both in the eastern and western
academies. In fact the West's attempt to manipulate the "Rushdie affair" by
valorizing a notion of secularism it so dearly cherished widened the already growing
gap between the two cultures. [7] The result was, as Ali Mazrui points out, a perfect
example of the dialogue of the deaf between the West and the world of Islam.
Mazrui writes: "the West was bewildered by the depth of Muslim anger. The
Muslims were bewildered by Western insensitivity. Was this yet another problem of
conflict of cultures" (*Cultural Forces,* 83)? Or could it be attributed to the problem
of (mis) translating an Eastern religiosity into a western context so that on the one
hand we have Muslims in Bradford, England, exploding with indignation, burning
copies of the book, declaring it to be *blasphemous* and on the other, a western
system of Law that upholds and protects freedom of speech and expression.

Among the many dismaying events that have occurred in the aftermath of the publication of Rushdie's novel; perhaps one particularly burdensome question has remained on the fringes of any discussion of *The Satanic Verses*. And this concerns the question of blasphemy itself. For by reading blasphemy solely in terms of religion, (as has been the characteristic trend of most discussions of *The Satanic Verses*), there is a subsequent **masking** of the other blasphemies that exist within Rushdie's novel. And by this I refer specifically to the portrayal of women in *The Satanic Verses*, for the female characters in Rushdie's novel do become the touchstones of blasphemic abuse. Thus, if the public contest between cultures has been privileged as a mode of reading the novel, the private violence against these fictional women has received little attention.

I believe, then, that one of the most problematic aspects of Rushdie's novel has been his anxiety to re-write or *translate* women into his narrative of postcolonial migration. By valorizing his two male protagonists' obsession with women and their desire to possess, control, and destroy them as a way of securing their own self-definition, Rushdie foregrounds the novel's fascination with violence and sexuality and his own ambivalent desire to tell stories and re-write segments of postcolonial history in the name of the woman.

One of the most interesting examples of Rushdie's ambivalence in the novel, is his attempt to *translate* or negotiate the story of Mahound in the name of the woman:

> Yet it must be acknowledged that in Mahound, we hear the satanic verses inspired by possible *female* gods. Gibreel's dream of Mahound's wrestling with himself, acting out an old script, restores the proper version, without the female angels, man to man. By the rules of fiction in the narrow sense you cannot assign the burden of responsibility here; although by the law of Religion, in the strict sense, the harm was already done. Rushdie invoked those rules against these laws, and it was an unequal contest. We will not enter the lists, but quietly mark the *text's* assignment of value. The "reality" of the wrestling, the feel of the voice speaking through one, is high on the register of validity, if not verifiability. By contrast in "Return to Jahilia," prostitution is mere play. Ayesha, the female prophet, ("historically" one of his wives) lacks the existential depth of "the businessman" prophet. To her the archangel sings in popular Hindi film songs. Her traffic with him is reported speech.[8]

Ayesha's sexuality in Rushdie's novel appears to be a commodity Mahound/Gibreel want to privatize and control. The novel's 'genderization of religion,' through the regulation of women's sexuality, then, becomes the touchstone of Gibreel's deluded fantasies, making these women the mutilated sites from which emerge a series of postcolonial histories of migration and dislocation.

If one of the central concerns of Rushdie's text is the role of blasphemy in a secular, postmodern world,[9] it would not be too far-fetched to claim that the blasphemies against the women characters in *The Satanic Verses* assume the intimacy of a new mode of translation whereby cultural complexities are rewritten within a framework of sexual ambiguity. In the context of such ambivalence, then, Rushdie engages with both the postcolonial self-definition and historiography, and the role of women in determining this historiography. However, I want to point out, that on such a score, *The Satanic Verses* is more outrageous and blasphemous to its women than to the most conservative Muslim. For Ayesha's "fatwa" or death sentence is announced long before Rushdie's:

> The explanation of this conundrum is to be heard, at this very moment, on certain surreptitious radio waves, on which the voice of the American convert Bilal is singing the Imam's holy song . . . Beginning with ritual abuse of the Empress, with lists of her crimes, murders, bribes, sexual relations with lizards, and so on, he proceeds eventually to issue in ringing tones the Imam's nightly call to his people to rise up against her evil State. 'We will make a revolution,' the Imam proclaims through him, 'that is a revolt not only against a tyrant, but against history.' For there is an enemy beyond Ayesha, and it is History herself. History is the blood-wine that must no longer be drunk. History the intoxicant, the creation and possession of the Devil, of the great Shaitan, the greatest of the lies—progress, science, rights— against which the Imam has set his face. History is a deviation from the Path, knowledge is a delusion . . . 'We will unmake the veil of history,' Bilal declaims into the listening night, 'and when it is unraveled, we will see paradise standing there, in all its glory and light . . . ' 'Death to the tyranny of the Empress Ayesha, of calendars, of America, of time! We seek the eternity, the timelessness of God. His still waters, not her flowing wines.'[10]

In this passage, Rushdie casts Ayesha as both History and Nation. She is the despot, the tyrant that must be destroyed.[11] She is the deviation from knowledge and truth and her deceptions need to be unveiled and unmade. However, even though Rushdie condemns her tyranny and the tyranny of superpowers and their fetishization of history in terms of linearity; he also criticizes the fundamentalist instinct to think of God in monolithic terms and contrasts this instinct with the non-linear, heterogeneous, even wayward instincts of Ayesha as history, as Nation. This is Rushdie's secularism speaking out against the impingement of a monolithic fundamentalism. Yet the internal dangers of Rushdie's text, his recreation of History and Nation in terms of Ayesha's excesses indicate Rushdie's fascination with the contest between the Imam and Ayesha, fundamentalism and secularism, linear and non-linear time, in terms of woman masquerading as History. For, Ayesha's body becomes the symbolic arena upon which Rushdie and his male narrators articulate their postcolonial dilemmas. Of course, the contest ends in what is fait accompli—the woman is destroyed, History is re-written in the name of the man, and Rushdie's ironic treatment of the fate of Ayesha (like all the other women in the novel) unmasks his own ambivalence towards women. Despite the plurality and secularity of *The Satanic Verses*, there is an underlying or masked aggression towards women in the novel that makes Rushdie's own position ambiguous. For, Rushdie's tirade against fundamental religion *translates* into aggression towards women.

Even his central character, Saladin Chamcha's revenge on Gibreel Farishta *translates* religious doubt into sexual doubt, "causing the trope of the satanic verses to return in its postmodern apparition as the anonymous and blasphemous telephone call" (*Rhetoric*, 196).

Saladin predicates his revenge by using the age-old trope of sexual jealousy. He does this by exploiting the body of Alleluia Cone, Gibreel's mistress, as the site for his own satanic prophecy:

> . . . it should be said that nobody, not Allie, not Gibreel, not even professional phone-tappers they brought in, ever suspected the calls of being a single man's work; but for Saladin Chamcha, once renowned (if only in somewhat specialist circles) as the man of a Thousand voices, such a deception was a simple matter, entirely lacking in effort or risk. In all, he was obliged to select (from his thousand voices and a voice) a total of no more than thirty nine.
>
> When Alice answered, she heard unknown men murmuring intimate secrets in her ear, strangers who seemed to know her body's most remote recesses, faceless beings who gave evidence of having learned, by experience, her choicest preferences among the myriad forms of love; and once the attempts at tracing the calls had begun her humiliation grew, because now she was unable simply to replace her receiver, but had to stand and listen, hot in the face and cold along the spine, making attempts (which didn't work) to actually prolong the calls.[12]

Blaspheming against sexual privacy, Saladin uses the female body to destroy his companion. For both these subcontinental men, to possess a European female body is a form of self-definition. However, while Saladin grows to understand the insufficiency of this, Gibreel is destroyed by his obsessive pursuit of the white woman's body. In the end, Saladin is reunited not with his mother but his father and his nationality, even though the ultimate consummation of his new/old identity is rendered in terms of a sexualized reunion with his Indian mistress Zeeny Vakil.

In articulating such a narrative of reunion and self-definition, Rushdie moves towards a version of *translating* a secular postcolonial saga of sexual relations in terms of *masquerade* where the drama of gender relations is disguised and re-presented in the form of religious historiography. However, while the gendering or sexualization of religion remains the burden of the 'Ayesha', and 'Return to Jahilia' episodes; the idea of women as sexualized spirits, transformed into vampires, over-sexed ghosts, insatiable prostitutes, and cold snow maidens persists throughout the novel. And, it is clear that these women are rendered strong only through their potential for violence. Like the surreal London of Gibreel's imagination, these protean, chameleon-like women lure people into states of exile, death or destruction.

My concern in this chapter, then, is to focus on Rushdie's portrayal in *The Satanic Verses* where I attempt to show that the stories of these women are rendered mute by Rushdie's re-rendering and re-gendering of a historico-religious narrative of exile and migration. Even though all these women, like the two male protagonists, Gibreel Farishta and Saladin Chamcha masquerade and assume different forms as a way of coping with marginalized situations; they remain prisoners of a violent narrative that compromises the subversive potentials of their masquerades. Ultimately, these women disintegrate into mutant forms that they cannot control, and it is through the exploitation of these women' masquerading bodies that the male protagonists attempt to invent temporary homelands and new identities.

Thus, if the blasphemy of the "Rushdie affair" in the eyes of the public has been submerged in East/West dichotomies and debates about free speech and fatwa; its re-citation within a feminist public discourse has been marginalized. It is my intention to engage with the sexual/textual politics of Rushdie's paradoxical desire to both incorporate 'woman' and exclude her from the history of postcolonial translation. But before I proceed to examine some of the interesting female characters in Rushdie's novel, I would like to dwell a little on the politics of postcolonial translation. In order to do this, it would be necessary to claim an indebtedness to Tejaswini Niranjana's theory of translation as disruption. According to Tejaswini Niranjana, translation has long been a site for perpetuating unequal relations between peoples, races, and languages. The traditional view of translation embraced by Western philosophy helped colonialism to recreate the exotic "other" as unchanging and outside history; in a complex field structured by law, violence, and subjectification. However, Niranjana writes that in the postcolonial context the problematic of translation becomes a significant site for raising questions about representation, power, and historicity:

> The context is one of contesting and contested stories attempting to account for, to recount, the asymmetry and inequality of relations between peoples, races, languages. Since the practices of subjection/subjectification implicit in the colonial enterprise operate not merely through coercive machinery of the imperial state but also through the discourses of philosophy, history, anthropology, philology, linguistics, and literary interpretation, the colonial "subject"—constructed through technologies or practices of power/knowledge—is brought into being within multiple discourses and on multiple sites. One such site is translation . . . Translation thus produces strategies of containment. By employing certain modes of representing the other—which it thereby also brings into being—translation reinforces the hegemonic versions of the colonized, helping them acquire the status of what Edward Said calls representations, or objects without history.[13]

Thus, translation attempts to fix colonized or marginalized subjects making them appear to be transparent, static and outside of history and by doing so renews or perpetuates new forms of domination. However, Niranjana points out that, since the Enlightenment, translation has also been used to understand modes of subjectification and such a rethinking has become the task of great importance and urgency for postcolonial theory that can, and must, reclaim the notion of translation by deconstructing it and reinscribing its potential as a strategy of resistance.

My concern is to explore this subversive potential of translation in Rushdie's novel by examining his use of masquerade with regard to the female characters in *The Satanic Verses*. In other words, does masquerade, as a strategy of postcolonial translation provide an effective means for the women in Rushdie's novel, particularly since the colonized woman exists only in translation, always already cathected by domination?

Since the crucial issue of postcolonial translation is disruption, it might be useful to see the extent to which Rushdie's translation of women in *The Satanic Verses* can be thought of as subversion or disruption. This is particularly important, because the novel loses some of its potential to subvert by not allowing its women to control their own masquerades. In Rushdie's novel, I believe, masquerade for a woman does not carry the potential for resistance. In postcolonial terms it does not produce a re-visioning process that enables these women to produce a narrative of their own and from a postcolonial critical perspective, their masquerades can be read as legacies of the colonial encounter. This is a condition of being both part of history, yet tyrannized by it, cut off from it, caught between a presence and absence in the condition of becoming anonymous, almost not invented in their own story.

Read as a form of postcolonial disruption, Rushdie's translation is rendered partially impotent by his inability to provide enabling strategies of masquerade for the women in his novel.

I would like to begin my reading of masquerade in *The Satanic Verses* with Ayesha's ineffectual masquerade as whore in the surreal, nightmarish scenes of the novel. Then, I will move on to discuss the transformation of Hind in the novel: Hind as the queen of Abu Simbel, and Hind in her reappearance as the wife of Muhammad Sufyan, the owner of the Brickhall Street café. I will conclude with some thoughts on other female characters in the novel— Pamela Lovelace, Zeeny Vakil, Rekha Merchant, Rosa Diamond, Alleluia Cone, and Ayesha of Titlipur, to suggest that all these women are versions or transformations of each other. As depictions of the homeland and Nationhood, these women are violated by both the narrative and through the imaginations of the male characters that render them powerless, disenfranchised, and on the peripheries of postcolonial narrative.

TRANSLATION AND MASQUERADE: THE ROLE(S) OF AYESHA-FAHISHA:

I would like to begin my discussion of Rushdie's representation of women in *The Satanic Verses* by proposing a link between the notions of *translation* and *masquerade*. By doing so I would like to suggest that Rushdie's ambivalent attempt to write women into the narrative of postcolonial history indicates a secular blasphemy that has received scant attention:

> In Salman Rushdie's novel the question arises whether he has libeled whole classes of Muslims— ranging from Shite believers . . . to the wives of the Prophet Muhammad.
>
> A related difficulty concerns the fact that Western Law provides very little protection against libel for those who are dead. If twelve women alive today were portrayed in a novel—under their own names—as the equivalent of prostitutes they would have some kind of legal recourse. But Rushdie is libeling women who have been dead some fourteen hundred years—the wives of Prophet Muhammad . . . [14]

While it is true that Rushdie translates Muhammad's wives into a secular narrative of debauchery and vice, it is also true that the prostitutes of 'The Curtain' masquerade as the prophet Mahound's wives. There is a double masquerade or a play within a play at work here, when Ayesha, as prostitute, transgresses the norms of feminine modesty and decorum by rewriting religious history to assume the identity of one of the prophet's wives as whore. By doing this she creates a new regime of power and profanity, growing so skillful in her masquerade that her previous self fades away. However, at another level, Ayesha's role-playing is controlled and explained by Salman the Persian as an ineffectual and pitiful effort to seek revenge on her husband:[15]

> He told Baal about a quarrel between Mahound and Ayesha, recounting the rumor as if it were incontrovertible fact. 'That girl couldn't stomach it that her husband wanted so many other women', he said. He talked about necessity, political alliances and so on, but she wasn't fooled. Who can blame her? Finally he went into—what else?— one of his trances, and out he came with a message from the archangel. Gibreel had recited verses giving him full divine support. God's own permission to fuck as many women as he liked. So there: what could poor Ayesha say against the verses of God . . . [16]

Here, Salman's translation or re-invention of Ayesha's quarrel with her husband transforms her into a figure of infidelity and doubt. Manipulated by a narrative that she cannot control, pitted against the words of Salman the scribe and God's own words transmitted by Gibreel, Ayesha's sexual excesses through her role playing and her attempts to get back at her husband are confined within the walls of the brothel. This renders her sexual prowess and her capacity to speak for herself captive and powerless, particularly when compared with the public storytelling role given to Salman the bard and the satanic archangel Gibreel. And, Salman continues to manipulate Ayesha through narrative corruption with his story of her indiscretion:

> Salman's story: Ayesha and the Prophet had gone on an expedition to a far-flung village, and on the way back to Yathrib their party had camped in the dunes for the night . . . At the last moment Ayesha was obliged by a call of nature to rush out of sight into a hollow . . . While she was away her litter-bearers picked up the palanquin and marched off. She was a light woman, and, failing to notice much difference in the weight of that heavy palanquin, they assumed she was inside. Ayesha returned after relieving herself to find herself alone, and who knows what

might have befallen her if a young man, a certain Safwan, had not chanced to pass by on a camel . . . The two young people had been alone in the desert for many hours, and it was hinted, more and more loudly, that Safwan was a dashingly handsome fellow . . . and might she not therefore have been attracted to someone closer to her own age? 'Quite a scandal,' Salman commented, happily.[17]

Salman's story about Ayesha's supposed sexual relationship with the young Safwan is a translation of an actual incident (the *ifk* incident) that is claimed to have occurred in the fifth or sixth year of the Islamic era. Michael Fischer and Mehdi Abedi write:

> In the fifth or the sixth year of the Islamic era, on the return from an expedition to the Banu Mustaliq, Ayesha, the youngest and most beloved wife of the Prophet, failed to reenter her closed palanquin at one of the rest stops, and was left behind. She was found by Safwan who escorted her back to the caravan. Allegations were raised about the compromising position she had allowed herself to be placed in. Muhammad had a revelation that cleared her of wrongdoing, and further proposed punishments for those who spread rumors and talk idly about chaste women. Revelations also imposed special conditions of concealment for the wives of the Prophet and even after the prophet's death no man would be allowed to marry his widows. Imam Ali, however, would not allow the issue to die, and he and Ayesha remained at odds. Imam Ali, and after him Muslim preachers, used the story to warn women against allowing any situation to arise in which even the appearance of the possibility of misdeeds could arise. Shi'ites in particular have seen Ayesha as a model of female transgression, rather than a model of a good Muslim woman; and Shi'ites often rhyme Ayesha's name with the word for whore, *fahisha*. No Shi'ite names his daughter Ayesha. Some women who live in a predominantly Shi'ite Iran, and who are given the name Ayesha, usually have another name which they use in public.[18]

Rushdie's reinscription of the *ifk* incident into the fabric of his fictional narrative performs the important task of re-historicizing an already narrated incident in terms of its status as fiction, whereby history is dismissed as fiction, but fiction, translated, is admissible as history. And this is done through the central motif of rumor and doubt where the credibility of Ayesha's integrity is at stake. Of course, in Salman's version of Ayesha's story, rumor is assigned the status of fact.

As a veiled allegory of the symbolic violence of historical process, the narrative of the "Brothel scene" acquires a freedom from factity in order to allegorize and fantasize a sequence of events at the expense of its central female character. Thus, the narrative in this scene founders on a excessive fictionality that it has been able to extract from historical discourse, and its tendency to hide behind the mask of allegory is emblematic of Rushdie's anxiety to translate women into the narrative of postcoloniality. This is because while the realism of the "original" incident is destablized by the re-invention of Salman's storytelling, Ayesha remains suspended in a condition of victim, not storyteller. She is tyrannized by Salman's imaginitive revisioning of *her* story.

While the revisioning of the *ifk* incident comes into dialectical play with its dominant version, attempting to generate new codes of reading and perception; it does so by silencing the marginal and dispossessed voice of Ayesha. As a consequence one is forced to ask the questions that Sara Suleri raises in her reading of Rushdie's novel *Shame*—"What must a text omit, in order that it may represent omission? What is the peculiar complicity between a radical ideology and a startlingly conservative need to take refuge in formalism" (*Rhetoric,* 175).

For this is a controversial episode in Rushdie's novel, where the narrative self-consciously undermines the "facts" of history by a variety of linguistic strategies in order to provide the structural freedom necessary to perform their own dramatic histories. In the brothel episodes, historical narrative is no longer chronicle, but Bilal's and Salman's clairvoyance. Thus, even though Ayesha is presented to us as historically constructed and connected; her sequel masquerade becomes an activity Bilal, Salman, Gibreel, and Rushdie wish to control and confine within the private spaces of the brothel. Eventually, the male characters display a vicarious pleasure in their attempts to publicize Ayesha's "shame". Salman's narrative license becomes an attempt to offer a definitive explanation for Ayesha's behavior rather than re-acquaint us with a history that has either erased women or done injustice to them.

This is a troubling section in Rushdie's novel particularly when read in the context of the Prophet's return to Jahilia (Mecca) where he introduces the rules and taboos of the new religion. However, these rules bring resistance or avoidance. Sexual licentiousness is rampant in the brothels, prayers to the old Gods are conducted in secret, pork is sold in the black market. In the midst of this diyonisiac frenzy, Rushdie incorporates the story of Ayesha, and the indictment of a whole town is articulated in terms of feminine transgression:

Hind and not Abu Simbel came to be thought of by Jahilians as the embodiment of the city, its living avatar, because they found . . . in the unflinching resolve of her proclamations as description of themselves far more palatable than the picture they saw in the mirror of Simbel's crumbling face. Hind's posters were more influential than any poet's verses. She was still sexually voracious, and had slept with every writer in the city . . . ; now the writers were used up, discarded, and she was rampant. With sword as well as pen. She was Hind, who had joined the Jahilian army disguised as a man, using sorcery to deflect all spears,.. Hind, who butchered the Prophet's uncle, and ate old Hamza's liver and his heart.[19]

Here Rushdie's narrative represents female sexuality in its most raw aspect, and the novel's fascination with female violence makes it complicit in the terrible aggression that it has sought to make solely the provenance of women. By equating female sexuality with textuality (Hind is both sexually and textually potent), the novel invests all the violence associated with Islamic historiography in its women until they literally *become* that violence, or at least an embodiment of it. Hind ravages the landscape of Jahilia:

> Who could resist her? . . . for these writings the people forgave her promiscuity, they turned a blind eye to the stories of Hind being weighed in emeralds on her birthday, they ignored rumors of orgies, they laughed when told of the size of her wardrobe, of the five hundred and eighty-one nightgowns made of gold leaf and the four hundred and twenty pairs of ruby slippers. The citizens of Jahilia dragged themselves through their increasingly dangerous streets, in which murder for small change was becoming commonplace, in which old women were being raped and ritually slaughtered, in which the riots of the starving were brutally put down by Hind's personal police force, the Manticorps; . . . [20]

Here Hind's sexual and material (allusions to Imelda Marcos are obvious) excesses seem to become the displaced centers of the narrative whereby Rushdie turns the trope of violence on women by transforming the woman into violator. However, Hind's potency is short lived. The Jahilian's abandon her in favor of Mahound:

> She screams at them, pleads, loosens her hair. 'Come to the house of the Black stone! Come and make sacrifice to Lat!' But they are gone . . . It is the end. The Grandee murmurs softly: 'Not many of us have reason to be scared of Mahound as you . . . [21]

But Hind is clever and deceptive. Disguising herself as a veiled woman she uses her sexuality and pretends to submit to the weak Mahound who welcomes her in his tents where she plots her revenge:

She locked herself in her tower room with a collection of ancient books written in scripts which no other human being in Jahilia could decipher . . . For two years and two months she saw no other living being. Then she entered her husband's bedroom at dawn . . . 'Wake up,' she commanded . . . 'It's a day for celebrations.' . . . 'What have we got to celebrate?' the former Grandee of Jahilia asked . . . Hind replied: 'I may not be able to reverse the flow of history, but revenge at least, is sweet.[22]

Within a few hours, the news of Mahound's fatal sickness spread in Jahilia. However, it seems to me that Hind's words in the above paragraph, "*I may not be able to reverse the flow of history, but revenge, at least, is sweet*" are crucial because they indicate an important dilemma that Rushdie is either unable to resolve or unwilling to resolve. This is the dilemma of granting agency to women to re-write and control or manipulate their own histories. For even though Hind is able to extract revenge (as Ayesha is able to lure the people of Titlipur to exile), she remains on the fringes of history, completely devoid of the textuality, ironically ascribed to her. And, this leaves her with nothing but the weapons of sorcery and sexuality. And the novel's continuous references to her "unchanging" nature, despite her reappearance in the form of Hind, the wife of Muhammad (Mahound) Sufyan, proprietor of the Shaandar Café must be read literally because in spite of her masquerades, Hind remains a static and alienated figure.[23]

In the guise of Muhammad Sufyan's wife, Hind becomes a trope for Hindustan, the land of the Hindus. While she is Islamicized by her relation with Mahound and Muhammad Sufyan, her battles with them can also be read as embodiments of communal violence and Hindu fundamentalism in India. Once again, woman becomes the emblem of dissonance and rivalry that disintegrates a unified myth of Nationhood. However, if Hind is the sexualized representation of a troubled Nation; she is also the image of Motherhood. But, in Hind's sexuality there lies a deeply oppressive paradox, because unlike her "other' versions, Abu Simbel's wife, or Ayesha the whore, Hind's sexual appetite is controlled and bounded through social custom and translated on to a culinary map:

And she devoured the highly spiced dishes of Hyderabad and the high-faluting yoghurt sauces of Lucknow her body began to alter, because all that food had to find a home somewhere, and she began to resemble the wide rolling land mass itself, the subcontinent without frontiers, because food passes across any boundary you care to mention . . . Restraint was not for Hind.[24]

However, predictably enshrined as the trope for motherhood and nation, Hind excludes all non-reproductively—oriented sexual relations with her husband:

> Ever since their marriage, the two of them had performed the sexual act infrequently, in total darkness, pin-drop silence and almost complete immobility. It would not have occurred to Hind to wiggle or wobble, and since Sufyan appeared to get through it all with an absolute minimum of motion, she took it . . . that the two of them were of the same mind on this matter, viz., that it was a dirty business . . . After this second daughter she told Sufyan that enough was enough, and ordered him to move his bed into the hall . . . but then she discovered that the lecher thought he could still, from time to time, enter her darkened room and enact that strange rite of silence and near-motionlessness to which she had submitted only in the name of reproduction. 'What do you think,' she shouted . . . 'I do this thing for *fun*?[25]

This problematic denial of female sexual pleasure in the case of Hind Sufyan, equates her sexuality with the responsibility of motherhood, and translates her body into a national landscape to be conquered and penetrated by male intrusion. Also, ironically, the marital discord between Hind and her husband is presented both as a metaphor for communal discord, and alienation from the homeland.[26]

Hind as Mother India submits both to the literal violation of her body as well as her metaphoric alienation from her lost homeland. She becomes the symbol of an alienated migrant and believes her life in England is a form of revenge that Muhammad bestows on her for refusing to participate in any sexual relations with him:

> . . . she was stuck forever in this England and would never see her village again. 'England,' she once said to him 'is your revenge on me for preventing you from performing your obscene acts upon my body' . . . Everything she valued had been upset by the change; had in this process of translation, been lost.[27]

Hind's potency both in the form of her sexual excesses as Abu Simbel's wife, and in the form of sexual restraint as Muhammad Sufyan's wife, is rendered ineffectual by the pathos of her alienation. Both versions of Hind remain lonely figures, on the outskirts of narrative agency.

Like Hind, Pamela Lovelace, Saladin Chamcha's English wife, is the embodiment of Nation—England, and it is by conquering her that Saladin attempts to re-invent his own identity as an Englishman:

Accelerating past Reading, Pamela gritted her teeth. One of the reasons she had decided to *admit it* and end her marriage before fate did it for her was that she had woken up one day and realized that Chamcha was not in love with her at all, but with that voice stinking of Yorkshire pudding and hearts of oak, that hearty, rubicund voice of ye olde dream England which he so desperately inhabits.[28]

Pamela's sterile relationship with Saladin is also marked by her inability to conceive and elevate her status from wife to mother so revered in Chamcha's India. Thus, Pamela's body becomes the barren embodiment of Chamcha's exile and despite their marriage and life in England, she can never make him *really belong*. Saladin realizes this (after his transformation into the fiendish goat) when he visits Pamela in their home and finds her living with his friend Jumpy Joshi. So, he turns to the "other" radical, rather breezy, and bohemian woman in his life—Zeeny Vakil from India. She is "a siren tempting him back to his old self" (*Satanic*, 58), constantly reminding him of his old Indian identity. In fact, when Saladin is with Zeeny he finds his earlier, submerged Indian self re-emerging. At first, he resents this. But in the end, when he is reunited with his dying father, Saladin is able to accept his India and "belong" or take refuge in Zeeny. Saladin's union with Zeeny is, once again, represented in the sexualized metaphor of orgiastic pleasure," 'I'm coming,' he answered her, and turned away from the view" (*Satanic,* 547). Once again, Rushdie's female character—this time the radical Zeeny Vakil, who is otherwise savvy, and political, can only come to life through her sexual union with Saladin. Saladin discovers that his masquerade of Englishness is not empowering and that he does not need either Zeeny or Pamela to define himself. He needs Zeeny only for a sexualized reassurance, that his new identity is safe, and can be reiterated again and again through the possession of her body.

Saladin's metamorphoses into the goat—devil is eventually therapeutic for him, and in the end his masquerades result in affirmation and reconciliation with his *father* and his homeland. This is the ethical aporia of Rushdie's novel. That Saladin Chamcha's evil masquerades, his destruction of Gibreel Farishta and Alleluia Cone, his malicious jealousy-inducing phone calls, enable him to survive, contrasts with the powerless masquerades of his female counterparts in the novel. In the words of Steven Walker, ". . . by the end of *The Satanic Verses* , Saladin Chamcha appears, not as a Raskolnikov in need of confession, penitence, punishment, and forgiveness, but rather as an ethically enigmatic figure who seems to have benefited from the evil he has done . . ." (*Magical*, 361).

Thus, Saladin continues to live on, and Gibreel gives in to death and self-destruction. However, Alleluia Cone and Rekha Merchant also bring upon Gibreel's destruction. They are Pamela and Zeeny's counterparts for Gibreel. While Rekha continuously reappears in the narrative as a siren, and vampire to haunt and torment Gibreel of his past, Allie is the cool English "snow maiden" who drives Gibreel to exile and destruction. In fact, throughout the novel, there are echoes of Allie in Rekha and vice-versa. Allie's obsessive desire to climb and conquer Mount Everest refers back to the Everest Vilas skyscraper in Bombay from which Rekha throws herself and her children, and Rushdie constantly draws parallels between the two as if they were representations or masquerades of each other:

> He made his escape. Alleluia, trying to follow him, was afflicted by such piercing pains in both feet that, having no option, she fell weeping on the floor: like an actress in a masala movie; or Rekha Merchant on the day Gibreel walked out on her for the last time.[29]

Here, their longing for Gibreel connects the two women to each other. The cinematic histrionics displayed by Alleluia is reminiscent of Gibreel's encounters with the dead actress, Rekha, who becomes his tormentor, and his nemesis. She drags him into the depths of despair and alienation—into the underworld of death, "'You don't know what hell is,' she snapped back, dropping the mask of her inperturbility. 'But buster, you sure will . . .'" (*Satanic*, 325).

Similarly, it is Gibreel's obsession with Allie that drives him to his final demise. Insane with jealousy at the thought of anyone else possessing her body, Gibreel succumbs to Saladin's phone calls and destroys both Allie and himself.

But contrary to Rekha's flamboyance and Hind's lack of restraint, Allie is presented as a cold, and virginal woman that Saladin immediately wants to destroy:

> The moment Saladin Chamcha got close enough to Allie Cone to be transfixed, and somewhat chilled by her eyes, he felt his reborn animosity toward Gibreel extending itself to her, with her degree—zero go-to-hell look, her air of being privy to some great, secret mystery of the universe; also her quality of what he would afterwards think of *wilderness*, a hard, sparse thing, anti-social, self-contained, an essence . . . Why, before she had opened her mouth, had he characterized her as part of the enemy?[30]

But Alleluia is hardly self-contained. She is a figment of both Gibreel and Saladin's inventions, and by inventing her as enemy, Saladin controls the fate of Alleluia. Through his obscene phone-calls, he plots her humiliation and eventual destruction. Allie becomes the victim of Saladin's vicious telephone narratives through which he regulates and manipulates her. And this is precisely because he both desires her and is incapable of dealing with her inner certainty:

> Perhaps because he desired her; and desired, even more, what he took to be that inner certainty of hers; lacking which, he envied it, and sought to damage what he envied . . . This happened: Chamcha invented an Allie, and became his fiction's antagonist . . . [31]

Yet, Allie performs her own masquerade. She is presented as the daughter of a Polish Jewish émigré and wartime survivor, who anglicized his name and conformed to the ways of English gentry. Allie, of course, reacts by rejecting all forms of imitation, accompanied by an acute desire to recover her own "true" heritage. And, this translates into a desire to re-situate herself within history, not outside of it, like her father. This, then, becomes Alleluia's reverse masquerade and translates into her tragicomic decision to renounce her old self and overcome her impending sense of catastrophe by climbing mountains and making history and re-casting herself as other and elsewhere. She decides to give up her licentious lifestyle and multitude of lovers:

> She admitted to him the early rumors about her unattainability, even frigidity, had some basis in fact. 'After Yel died, I took on her side as well.' . . . 'Plus I really wasn't enjoying it anymore. It was mostly revolutionary socialists at the time, making do with me while they dreamed about some heroic women they'd seen on their three-trips to Cuba. Never touched *them*, of course; the combat fatigues and ideological purity scared them silly. They came home humming "Guantanamera" and rang me up.' She opted out. 'I thought let the best minds of my generation soliloquize about power over some other woman's body, I'm off.' She began climbing mountains . . . 'because I knew they'd never follow me up there. But then I thought bullshit. I didn't do it for them; I did it for me.[32]

Ironically enough, though, Alleluia uses her body as the vehicle to overcome her sexual exploitation by men. In her recurring obsession to climb Mount Everest without oxygen, experiencing as much pain and difficulty as possible; Allie attempts to subsume her sexual drive and recreate herself into a spiritual and elusive woman. However, even if spirituality and sexuality merge in Allie's desire to climb mountains; her spirituality is subsumed in favor of sexuality in the imagination of both male protagonists. Her relationship with Gibreel is explosive and re-kindles that sexual appetite once again and makes her feel "invaded or potentially invaded . . ." (*Satanic*, 300). With Saladin she becomes the target of voyeuristic and blasphemous fantasies. Saladin possesses Allie vicariously through Gibreel's re-rendering of their private, sexual relationship, and once again the mask of Allie as ice queen, hard, and cold is rekindled in the imaginings of both Gibreel and Saladin's vile fantasies. For Gibreel, the possession of Allie's body becomes a way of taking refuge and achieving self-definition. No longer the beloved movie idol of Bollywood, Gibreel leaves his past behind in order to conquer Alleluia Cone and gain reassurance of his own identity. But in his imaginings Allie is represented as a false temptress through whom he cannot regain any form of certainty. As Gibreel wanders around the surreal and nightmarish landscape of a protean and metamorphosed city, he makes a connection between the stifling and angry masks of the city and the fiendish masquerade of Alleluia, making her the embodiment of the city's "true. capricious, tormented nature," (*Satanic*, 320). He imagines and invents Alleluia as:

> O most false of creatures! O princess of the powers of the air! . . . what had Alleluia done for him? *You are not yourself. I don't think you are really well.* —O bringer of tribulation, creatrix of strife, of soreness of the heart! Siren, temptress, fiend in human form! That snowlike body with its pale, pale hair; how she had used it to fog his soul, and how hard he had found it . . . to resist
> . . . Enmeshed by her in the web of a love so complex . . . He had come to the very edge of the ultimate Fall . . . How beneficent, then, the Over-Entity had been to him!—He saw now that the choice was simple: the infernal love of the daughters of men, or the celestial adoration of God.[33]

For Saladin, Allie becomes a means of destroying Gibreel, and his conquest of her is played out in his reinvention of her as a woman defamed, as a fallen woman conducting secret sexual liaisons with other men. Thus, Allie's invention by Saladin and Gibreel make her into a tragicomic, mutant masquerader who succumbs to and is destroyed by her male counterparts. In fact, Allie's masquerade is interrupted and rendered ineffectual by Saladin's invention and Gibreel's imaginings of her as a protean siren in human form that uses her sexual charms and mask of unattainibility to capture him. So, instead of reclaiming for her, through masquerade, a place in history lost by her father she turns into a mass of body conquered by the paranoid imaginings of Saladin Chamcha and Gibreel Farishta.

Like Allie, Rosa Diamond, the eighty-eight year old widow of an Argentinean, near whose house Gibreel and Saladin land after their fall from the highjacked plane *Bostan*, is also wrapped up in dreams of being elsewhere and other. Rosa inhabits the most surreal chapters of Rushdie's novel. Enmeshed in a dream-like narrative, Rosa represents yet another version of that elusive "real" England that Saladin and Gibreel so desire. In fact their landing on her property is reminiscent of a conquest, another invasion by William the Conqueror, except that, whereas the Norman fleet came sailing openly, these men arrive sneakily: " 'What do you imagine yourselves to be doing here?' Death wanted to know. 'This is private property. There's a sign' " (*Satanic*, 132).

However, not only is Rosa lost in the reveries of her past, she imposes these memories on her captives and imprisons Gibreel with her death-like trance and gift for spinning extraordinary stories of violent feuds in the colonial Argentinean society she belonged to. With Rosa, Rushdie inverts the colonial paradigm by casting her as England, the conqueror, and the male figures she interacts with, as the conquered. By initiating this reversal of roles, Rushdie invokes England's nostalgia for lost empires (India, Pakistan, and the Falklands).

But, Rosa as conqueror can only survive through her metamorphosed reveries of sexual combat and historical memory. Her masquerade as history is always translated in terms of sexual memory. Her whole reason for living is to remember if she did, in fact, have sexual relations with her Argentinean lover, and her own longings for him are translated in her fantastical stories of the feuds of the beautiful Claudette, Aurora del Sol, and Martin de la Cruz.

Rosa's power as conqueror, and narrator of history is eventually impotent. Even though she momentarily mesmerizes Gibreel, Rosa's dream of possessing Argentina through her imprisonment of Gibreel cannot be realized. And, as the apparitions in her stories gain clarity, Rosa, herself, " grew fainter and fainter, fading away, exchanging places . . . with ghosts" (*Satanic*, 153).

Rosa's narrative gradually degenerates into uncertainty and confusion and in the end, when she is dying, she is not able to keep her dreams alive. Her narrative confusion is translated into sexual doubt and she is unable to decide if she did, in fact, possess Argentina through a sexualized union with Martin de la Cruz. In fact she is not able to remember if she had any sexual relations with him at all—" the two possibilities kept alternating, while the dying Rosa tossed on her bed, did-she-didn't- she, making the last version of the story of her life, unable to decide what she wanted to be true" (*Satanic*, 152).

Rosa's narrative confusion undermines her credibility and status as storyteller and as the emblem of English history. Eventually, Gibreel is able to save himself from her narrative sorcery by explaining away her powers as the remnants "of the faded grandeur of an extinct species" (*Satanic*, 144). Thus, the colonizing nation is destroyed in its feminine form and the colonized nation in its male manifestation is able to escape her deceptions and imprisonment.

Gibreel leaves Rosa after she dies and wanders through London in search of his other nemesis, Alleluia Cone. His mesmerization with Rosa translates into his paranoid and deluded obsession with Allie. Saladin, however, is taken away by the immigration authorities as an illegal alien and he begins his transformation into a fiendish goat-devil which, ironically, enables him to reacquaint himself with his Indian identity.

If Rosa Diamond's masquerade as history and nation is represented in secular terms, Ayesha's metamorphosis from the goddess Al-Lat of Jahilia, and the whore of 'The Curtain', into the enigmatic butterfly woman of Titlipur is rendered as a translation of history in the name of woman through a religious episode. The "Ayesha" section in *The Satanic Verses* is based on multiple events in postcolonial history and is retold in the spirit of a folk tale. It echoes the famous Hawkes Bay case that occurred in Pakistan in 1983. It also recalls the nationalistic Dundee Salt March led by Mahatma Gandhi in India in the 1940's, where a large section of the Indian population marched to Dundee on the coast of Gujarat, to collect and make salt to protest the new salt laws imposed on them by the British. It also refers us to the Biblical episode of the Exodus where the parting of the Red Sea allowed Moses and his followers to cross the waters on foot.[34]

The Ayesha episode is also a retelling of the episode of the satanic verses through the woman where Ayesha replaces Mahound and becomes the recipient of the archangel's message. The blasphemy of this episode in its multiple translations of stories of Nationhood, exile, and protest, is reformulated by Rushdie through his use of the tropology of Islam. But, Islam in its feminine masquerade, through Ayesha, is not an enabling conceit. The narrative, by assuming the highly ambitious task of translating Islam through the masquerade of Ayesha, renders Ayesha, not to be the bearer of God's message, but the devil's. Ayesha is the sorceress who leads the innocent people of Titlipur to death. And, even though she represents the fusion of God and devil, as does Gibreel, her masquerade is trivialized by her playful sexuality, and contrasts with the "seriousness" of the businessman Mahound's message to the people of Jahilia. Also, Ayesha attains the status of Prophet by her sexual indiscretions with the archangel whom she lures into her web of deceit. Finally, it is never clear if Ayesha's message is indeed the message of the archangel.

Not only does Ayesha entice the archangel, but also unlike Mahound, she is represented as a being without any conscience, without any struggle:

With Mahound, there is always a struggle; with the Imam, slavery; but with this girl, there is nothing. Gibreel is inert, usually asleep in the dream as he is in life. She comes upon him under a tree, or in a ditch, hears what he isn't saying, takes what she needs, and leaves.[35]

If Ayesha is rendered powerful in her disguise as the Prophet; her masquerade as the butterfly woman is rendered ineffectual by Mirza Saeed who views her as a potential threat. In his alternating attraction and paranoid fear of her, he is convinced that she must be destroyed, and he attempts to do this by controlling her sexuality through his own fantasies. However, for Mirza, Ayesha's presence in the village, and in his own house as his wife's new best friend, turns into a potential threat. Mirza's efforts to re-kindle his sexual desires for his wife, through his fantasies of Ayesha, lead him to play games. He asks Mishal, his wife, to confine herself to her Zenana hoping that this form of confinement would result into a new and renewed sexual desire. However, Mirza is not able to control Mishal because Ayesha joins her in the Zenana and begins to exert an extraordinary power over her. The confined space of the Zenana, then, turns into a space of transgression and female friendship.[36]

When Ayesha lures the entire village to a pilgrimage to Mecca, leading them to ambivalent disaster, Mirza is determined to unmask her dubiety. However, he is not able to convince the people of Titlipur not to succumb to her deceptions, and it is only at the very end, that the Imam, Ayesha's tempter and old antagonist is able to undo her. Through her symbolic death, the miracle of the parting of the waters takes place:

> Then the sea poured over him, and he was in the water beside Ayesha, who had stepped miraculously out of his wife's body . . . 'Open', she was crying . . . Tentacles of light were flowing from his body and he chopped at them, chopped, using the side of his hand . . . He was a fortress changing gates . . . He was drowning.-She was drowning, too. He saw the water fill her mouth, heard it begin to gurgle in her lungs. Then something within him refused that, made a different choice, and at that instant . . . he opened. His body split apart . . . so that she could reach deep within him . . . and at that moment of their opening the waters parted . . . [37]

Here the idea of miracle is based on the sexualized possession of the deceptive woman. The narrative control in the episode above is clearly in the hands of the Imam *who chooses sex instead of death* for Ayesha. Gibreel who speaks to her, flippantly, only in the idiom of popular Hindi songs trivializes Ayesha's prophecy from the start. The language of uncertainty that informs her prophecy and characterizes her masquerade as butterfly woman, "Everything is required of us, and everything will be given" (*Satanic*, 235), becomes the embodiment of exile, and is rendered false and mute by the disastrous finale of the pilgrimage that she leads.

* * *

Turning back to the question of Rushdie's use of female masquerade in *The Satanic Verses* as a strategy for translating woman into the narrative of postcoloniality, I would like to point out that in mostly every case, the masquerading female in the novel, is controlled and manipulated by the narrative of male authority. The image of woman as nation and culture woven into the fabric of Rushdie's postcolonial narration grants her limited agency. Ravaged by an ambivalent discourse, the power of her masquerade is rendered ineffectual.

In the case of Rosa or Ayesha, who are allowed to be at the center of their narratives, Rushdie undercuts their potential for power by not allowing them to survive, even in translation. Their hybridity is restricted and since "hybridity leads to proliferating differences that escape the "surveillance" of the discriminatory eye . . . to restrict "hybridity." Or what I call "living in translation . . ." (*Siting*, 46) is to deny the complete realization of the power of masquerade or heterogeneous transformations:

> Hybridity can be seen, therefore, as the sign of a post-colonial theory that subverts essentialist models of reading while it points to a new practice of translation.[38]

While Rushdie's attempts to re-translate and re-historicize in the name of women by problematizing the issue of representation, which is crucial in a context where nationalist myths of identity and unity are collapsing, is a point well taken; he is not able to destabilize the "original" by first unmasking what is presented as "natural". In other words, by historicizing women through a re-writing of religious and nationalist discourse, Rushdie opens the door for his female characters to enter the narrative from the peripheries. He is unable to fully dissociate their representations from the existent, dominant tropes that objectify them, and *The Satanic Verses*, itself becomes a mask for feminine objectification.

As postcolonials we already exist in translation. It is extremely important, then, to transform translation into a disruptive and disseminating force because "the deconstruction" initiated by re-translation opens up a post-colonial space that can bring different histories to legibility.

Rushdie recognizes this and continues to be preoccupied with this problem in the novels that followed. In *The Moor's Last Sigh* the Aurora del Sol of Rosa's narrative reappears as the eccentric Aurora da Gama Zogoiby who is finally able to take over the narrative from the peripheries, even though she does not, actually, narrate her own story. However, the tropes that characterize women in *The Satanic Verses* reappear in this novel in the form of Uma Sarasvati metamorphosed into an avenging angel who undercuts the power of Aurora. Woman's masquerade is once again rendered ineffectual, and its potential to subvert is compromised. The question that arises, then, is, can women use masquerade as a form of resistance? In the next chapter Pratibha Parmar attempts to address this question through the representations of women's masquerades in her videos.

NOTES

1. Salman Rushdie, *The Moor's Last Sigh* (London: Jonathan Cape, 1995) 309–310.

2. Salman Rushdie, *The Satanic Verses* (New York: Viking, 1988) 206.

3. Tejaswini Niranjana, *Siting Translation: History, Post-Structuralism, and the Colonial Context* (Berkeley: U of California P, 1992) 1.

4. Salman Rushdie, *Shame* (New York: Vintage, 1989) 189.

5. Tejaswini Niranjana, *Siting Translation: History, Post-Structuralism, and the Colonial Context* (Berkeley: U of California P, 1992) 172–173.

6. Ania Loomba, *Colonialism/Postcolonialism* (London and New York: Routledge, 1998) 215.

7. Many intellectuals of Indian origin have criticized Western notions of secularism. Ranajit Guha and the Subaltern Studies group points out the inability of western orientalists to think about insurgent mentality except in terms of pure and unadulterated secularism,. Dipesh Chakraborty aligns the case against secularism with a case against Indian elitist nationalists who by means of an act of appropriation use secular nationalism as a means of building an Indian state. In his reading of the work of Edward Said, R.Radhakrishnan believes that Said concedes to the secular imagination and by doing so overlooks and trivializes native and indigenous ways of doing and living knowledge. According to other critics of western centered secularists, the notion of the secular is the product of the Enlightenment whereby a sharp distinction is made between the irrational, religious behavior of the Orient and the rational secularism of the West. See, R.Radhakrishnan, "Edward Said's *Culture and Imperialism*: A Symposium *Social Text* 40 (1994): 15–20, and Ranajit Guha and Gayatri Chakravorty Spivak, eds. *Selected Subaltern Studies* (New York: Oxford UP, 1988).

8. Gayatri Chakravorty Spivak, *Outside in the Teaching Machine* (New York and London: Routledge, 1993) 224.

9. See Gayatri Chakravorty Spivak, "Reading *The Satanic Verses*," *Outside in the Teaching Machine* (New York and London: Routledge, 1993) 217–241, and Sara Suleri, "Salman Rushdie: Embodiments of Blasphemy, Censorships of Shame," *The Rhetoric of English in India* (Chicago: U of Chicago P, 1992) 174–206.

10. Salman Rushdie, *The Satanic Verses* (New York: Viking, 1988) 210–211.

11. It is interesting that Rushdie represents Ayesha's tyranny in the context of first world (America) domination. The forced connection between third world woman and American aggression *unmasks* Rushdie's own ambivalence towards women. In this passage Ayesha is not only represented in terms of History and Nation, but is recast as a *masquerading* devil. Perhaps Bilal's antagonism parodies Rushdie's own complicated fascination/revulsion towards his female characters, particularly in his own desire to "unveil" and unmake History.

12. Salman Rushdie, *The Satanic Verses* (New York: Viking, 1988) 443–444.

13. Tejaswini Niranjana, *Siting Translation: History, Post-Structuralism and the Colonial Context* (Berkeley: U of California P, 1992) 1–3.

14. Ali Mazrui, *Cultural Forces in World Politics* (London: Heinemann, 1990) 88.

15. It is interesting that the storyteller who ultimately renders Ayesha's powerful masquerades ineffectual through the power of his words and role as scribe is called Salman! The ultimate power of the author over his creations is apparent here and in a way indicates Rushdie's own authority as writer to manipulate his characters.

16. Salman Rushdie, *The Satanic Verses* (New York: Viking, 1988) 386.

17. Salman Rushdie, *The Satanic Verses* (New York: Viking, 1988) 387.

18. Michael Fischer and Mehdi Abedi, "Postscriptural Paregon: Bombay Talkies, the Word and the World, Salman Rushdie's *The Satanic Verses*," *Debating Muslims,* (Madison: U of Wisconsin P, 1990) 416.

19. Salman Rushdie, *The Satanic Verses* (New York: Viking, 1988) 360–361.

20. Salman Rushdie, *The Satanic Verses* (New York: Viking, 1988) 361.

21. Salman Rushdie, *The Satanic Verses* (New York: Viking,1988) 372.

22. Salman Rushdie, *The Satanic Verses* (New York: Viking, 1988) 393.

23. Hind's sterile masquerades are important because they are different from the active metamorphoses of the novel's two central characters—Saladin Chamcha and Gibreel Farishta. Although *The Satanic Verses* has received attention for giving rise to a confrontation between Islamic fundamentalism and Western secularism; it is a novel about *masquerade* and the way in which masquerade operates as a central motif in assigning identities within the postcolonial context. The immigrant Other in the novel changes in several ways. Sometimes the metamorphosis is degrading, sometimes phantasmagorical.

24. Salman Rushdie, *The Satanic Verses* (New York: Viking, 1988) 246.

25. Salman Rushdie, *The Satanic Verses* (New York: Viking, 1988) 247–248.

26. Abu Simbel (Egypt) and Hind (India) allude to the enmity between Hindus and Muslims. This is also apparent in Hind's rivalry with both Mahound and Muhammad.

27. Salman Rushdie, *The Satanic Verses* (New York: Viking, 1988) 248–249.

28. Salman Rushdie, *The Satanic Verses* (New York: Viking, 1988) 180.

29. Salman Rushdie, *The Satanic Verses* (New York: Viking, 1988) 319.

30. Salman Rushdie, *The Satanic Verses* (New York: Viking, 1988) 428.

31. Salman Rushdie, *The Satanic Verses* (New York: Viking, 1988) 428.

32. Salman Rushdie, *The Satanic Verses* (New York: Viking, 1988) 312–313.

33. Salman Rushdie, *The Satanic Verses* (New York: Viking, 1988) 321.

34. The Hawkes Bay case took place in Pakistan when thirty-eight Shia Muslims walked into the Arabian Sea expecting the waters to part. A woman called Naseem Fatima who claimed to be the direct visionary of the twelfth Imam inspired them. See Akbar Ahmad, *Pakistan Society: Islam, Ethnicity, and Leadership in South Asia* (Karachi: Oxford UP, 1986) 46–67. As far as the Dundee March is concerned, it is interesting to note that thousands of women participated in the march, even though Gandhi refused to let them participate. See Ketu Katrak, "Indian Nationalism, Female Sexuality," in *Nationalisms and Sexualities*, ed. Andrew Parker (New York and London: Routledge, 1992) 400. In the context of Rushdie's novel, then, this recasting of Ayesha as Gandhi, leader of the March, is indeed a subversive strategy.

35. Salman Rushdie, *The Satanic Verses* (New York: Viking, 1988) 234.

36. It is interesting that the Mirza's house in Titlipur is not only the biggest and the best but is constructed and designed on the model of homes built by a prominent English architect. However, the creation of a zenana within an otherwise modern space, is an interesting spatial contradiction that Rushdie incorporates in his novel.

37. Salman Rushdie, *The Satanic Verses* (New York: Viking, 1988) 506–507)

38. Tejaswini Niranjana, *Siting Translation: History, Post-Structuralism, and the Colonial Context* (Berkeley: U of California P, 1992) 46.

CHAPTER THREE

The Voices of Masquerade: The Representation of Subalternity in Two Videos by Pratibha Parmar

One never encounters the testimony of the woman's voice-consciousness. Such a testimony would not be ideology—transparent or "fully" subjective, of course, but it would have constituted the ingredients for producing a counter-sentence. As one goes down the grotesquely mistranscribed names of these women . . . one cannot put together a "voice." The most one can sense is an immense heterogeneity . . . [1]

In this chapter I will discuss the *masquerade* of subaltern women with reference to questions of agency and *voice*. Here, I use Gayatri Chakravorty Spivak's idea of the *subaltern as organic intellectual* [2] to read women's masquerade and activism in *Sari Red* and *Khush*, two films by Asian/British film and video artist, Pratibha Parmar. Since most racial formulations of masquerade derived from dominant theoretical traditions simply substitute the position of the white woman for the postcolonial, the voices and testimony of the subaltern woman remains either submerged or simply outside the realm of discourse.[3] Does this mean that the subaltern woman cannot be an active participant in her own discourse formation? Or does it mean, as bell hooks has pointed out, that it is very difficult to theorize the position of the colored woman within current paradigms?

These and other questions are addressed in the independent videos of Asian/British filmmaker Pratibha Parmar. Read in conjunction with Spivak's polemical and much debated essay, " Can the Subaltern Speak?", these videos are examples of an emerging counterculture that uses media to create spaces within which different forms of cultural and political activism can be articulated. By undermining and subverting the "authority" of mainstream, patriarchal theorizing (both Eurocentric and non-Eurocentric) and by positioning audiovisual culture as a positive alternative; Parmar's films have tipped the scales of "high" versus "low", elite versus mass culture in interesting ways. By addressing the Asian woman's experiences of racism and sexism in Britain, Parmar foregrounds the resistances and struggles set up by these women. By rejecting existing signifying practices, Parmar shifts the paradigm of masquerade by altering, displacing, and disrupting its modes of articulation to include the challenge presented by the heterogeneous voices of subalternity.

As a woman and feminist, it is impossible for me not to recognize in the voices of Parmar's women, a certain strength marked by an unmitigated energy that celebrates and validates their existence. These women do not speak from a position of marginalization but from a position of **resistance**. They speak for themselves. In this sense, their discourse runs counter to Spivak's position in her essay, "Can the Subaltern Speak?", that the "female subaltern **cannot** speak." However, Spivak's rejection of any simplistic desire to let the native speak in order to counter the discourses of domination must only be read in the context of her critique of the various accounts of *Sati* or widow burning in the "multiple determinations of archival sources" found in the police reports, or in the records of the East India Company, where ". . . the task of recovering a (sexually) subaltern subject is lost in an institutional textuality at the archaic origin."[4] Here the subaltern subject is either lost or overdetermined. The profound irony in locating or recovering the voice of the subaltern, according to Spivak is that:

> Between patriarchy and imperialism, subject- constitution and object-formation, the figure of the woman disappears, not into a pristine nothingness, but into a violent shuttling which is the displaced figuration of the "third-world woman" caught between tradition and modernization.[5]

This passage echoes the irony of Spivak's position vis-à-vis the subaltern woman. Critiquing dominant notions of voice as the index of a present and powerful subject, Spivak vehemently opposes any possibility of recovering a clear and transparent "voice" of the oppressed woman. And this, she dramatizes in her reading of Bhuvaneswari Baduri's story:

> A young woman of sixteen or seventeen, Bhuvaneswari Baduri, hanged herself in her father's modest apartment in North Calcutta in 1926. The suicide was a puzzle since, as Bhuvaneswari was menstruating at the time, it was clearly not an illicit pregnancy. Nearly a decade later, it was discovered that she was a member of one

of the many groups involved in the armed struggle for Indian independence. She had finally been entrusted with a political assassination.

Unable to confront the task and yet aware of the practical need for trust, she killed herself . . . Bhuvaneswari had known that her death would be diagnosed as the outcome of illegitimate passion. She had therefore waited for the onset of menstruation.[6]

Spivak proceeds to analyze Bhuvaneswari's suicide. I quote her at length:

While waiting, Bhuvaneswari, the *brahmacarini* who was no doubt looking forward to good wifehood, perhaps rewrote the social text of *sati*-suicide in an interventionist way . . . She generalized the sanctioned motive for female suicide by taking immense trouble to displace (not merely deny), in the physiological inscription of her body, its imprisonment with legitimate passion by a single male. In the immediate context, her act became absurd, a case of delirium rather than sanity. The displacing gesture— waiting for menstruation—is at first a reversal of the interdict against a menstruating widow's right to immolate herself; the unclean widow must wait, publicly, until the cleansing bath of the fourth day, when she is no longer menstruating, in order to claim her dubious privilege. In this reading, Bhuvaneswari Baduri's suicide is an unemphatic, ad hoc, subaltern rewriting of the social text of *sati*-suicide as much as the hegemonic account of the blazing, fighting, familial Durga. The emerging dissenting possibilities of the hegemonic account of the fighting mother are well documented and popularly well remembered through the discourse of the male leaders and participate in the independence movement. The subaltern as female cannot be heard or read.

I know of Bhuvaneswari's life and death through family connections. Before investigating them more thoroughly, I asked a Bengali woman, a philosopher and Sanskritist whose early intellectual production is almost identical to mine, to start the process. Two responses: (a) Why, when her two sisters, Saileswari, and Raseswari, led such full and wonderful lives, are you interested in the hapless Bhuvaneswari? (b) I asked her nieces. It appears that it was a case of illicit love.[7]

Bhuvaneswari's "voice", her act of displacement or resistance—her deliberate decision to wait for the onset of menstruation so that her suicide is not read as an act of desperation, or an attempt to mask traces of a prohibitory love affair or illicit pregnancy, is systematically erased by the stories and memories of family members and male freedom fighters. It is only through Spivak's interventionist re-reading of Baduri's unfortunate story that we are able to extricate the female subaltern's "voice" on its own terms. However, I believe that Spivak's re-rendition of Bhuvaneswari's suicide, although significant, is a circumscribed act of interpretation. While Spivak's conclusion that "the subaltern cannot speak" does not reflect a political and strategical pessimism; she does not create a discursive space from which Bhuvaneswari is able to articulate her story on her own terms. I am not sure if this can be read as a categorical denial of voice to the subaltern so that she can only be spoken for; but I am certain that the task of the postcolonial feminist is not limited to speak on behalf of the marginalized woman. She must create a space from which she is allowed to speak for herself. It is crucial for postcolonial women writers, artists, activists, and theorists to be cognizant of this difference.

I reiterate, Bhuvaneswari is not ultimately a subject of resistance. Even though she uses her sexualized, gendered body to contradict what she knew would be the dominant interpretation of her act of suicide, her counter-discourse is neither heard nor read because it is *circumscribed* by the boundaries of its own gender identity. Spivak confronts the severity of this in the introduction to her translation of the stories of Bengali writer Mahasweta Devi published in 1995:

> . . . One of the bases in women's subalternity (and indeed in unequal gendering on other levels of society) is internalized constraints seen as responsibility, and therefore the very basis of gender-ethics. Here women's separation from organic intellectuality is a complicity with gendering that cannot not be perceived by many as sweetness, virtue, innocence, simplicity. If in the case of Bhuvaneswari ("Can the Subaltern Speak?") and Jashoda in Mahasweta's "Stanadayini", it is parts of the sexed body . . . that are invested with meaning . . . internalized gendering perceived as ethical choice is the hardest roadblock for women the world over. The recognition of male exploitation must be supplemented with this acknowledgement. And the only way to break it is by establishing an ethical singularity with the woman in question, itself a necessary supplement to a collective action to which the woman might offer resistance, passive or active.[8]

Two crucial and interconnected notions emerge in this passage—"ethical singularity", and "organic intellectual". The concept of "ethical singularity" is basic to intellectuality and collective action. Spivak writes:

> "Ethical singularity" is neither "mass contact" nor engagement with "the common sense of the people." We all know that when we engage profoundly with one person, the responses come from both sides: this is responsibility and

accountability. We also know that in such engagements we want to reveal and reveal, conceal nothing. Yet on both sides there is always a sense that something has not got across. This we call the "secret," not something that one wants to conceal, but something that one wants to reveal . . . In this secret singularity, the object of ethical action is not an object of benevolence . . . It is not identical with the frank and open exchange between radicals and the oppressed in times of crisis, or the intimacy that the anthropologists often claim with their informant groups, although the importance of at least the former should not be minimized. This encounter can only happen when the respondents inhabit something like normality. Most political movements fail in the long run because of the absence of this engagement. In fact it is impossible for all the leaders (subaltern or otherwise) to engage every subaltern in this way, especially across the gender divide. This is why ethics is the experience of the impossible. Please note that I am not saying that ethics are impossible, but rather that ethics is the experience of the impossible. This understanding only sharpens the sense of the crucial and continuing need for collective political struggle. For a collective struggle *supplemented* by the impossibility of full ethical engagement . . . [9]

Spivak points out that no amount of consciousness raising can come close to the "painstaking labor to establish ethical singularity with the subaltern" (Imaginary, 25). In order to become "organic intellectuals", it is necessary for the subaltern woman to be aware of this impossibility and not be complicit with any overt forms of gendering. This is crucial, because,, like the case of Bhuvaneswari Baduri, a gender specific act of resistance cannot be read or understood on its own terms. Baduri's ethical choice is expressed only when her gender specific internalized constraints are explained not as limitations but as acts of resistance that are not defined by dominant, patriarchal codes. And this can only be possible through acts of reading. The subaltern woman can only be spoken for!

Does this mean, then, that it is impossible for one to maintain solidarity with the subaltern on her own terms? Or does it mean, as Spivak suggests, that one way to establish an ethical relationship with the subaltern is by way of intellectuality?

The idea of the "organic intellectual" is basic to Spivak's evolving feminist, political, and theoretical speculations. Originally presented by Gramsci in *Prison Notebooks* to signify: "Every social group, coming into existence on the original terrain of an essential function in the world of economic production creates together with itself, organically, one or more strata of intellectuals which give it homogeneity and an awareness of its own function not only in the economic but also in the social and political fields" (*Prison*, 5)., Spivak reuses the term within the context of an entirely different history—the history of tribal India where she believes it is possible to elaborate the existence of an "organic intellectual" as opposed to the Italian context where Gramsci, himself, believed it was not possible for such an intellectual to exist. This was because it was important for the Italian peasant to first go through traditional education before he could enter the realm of intellectuality.

With the case of India, Spivak believes this has happened because some of the denotified Indian tribes have been able to separate themselves from the mainstream peasants to produce intellectuals like Jaladhar Sabar whose education Spivak points out, has been his association with Mahasweta Devi, herself a female organic intellectual of "unusual ethical responsiveness."[10] She is ". . . the new intellectual that can no longer consist in eloquence . . . but in active participation in practical life, as constructor, organizer . . ." (*Prison*, 10). Spivak's "organic intellectual," then, is not an elaboration of identity so much as an emphasis on the intellectual's function. Here the word "class" loses its potency because organic intellectuals are created in every class and can work together collectively.

If the "class" factor seems to disappear (or exist in metonymic collectivity) from Spivak's "organic intellectual;" it is possible for the subaltern woman to enter the realm of intellectuality in order to "speak" rather than be spoken for. From this I conclude that it is possible for her to break down the barriers of her own internalized and gender specific constraints to articulate an ethical choice—a precursor for any form of collective action.[11]

* * *

I would now like to turn to the field of cultural activism whose development both intersects and runs parallel to Spivak's theoretical interventions. Spivak's position, reiterated through the text "Can the Subaltern Speak?" that the "female subaltern cannot speak" but can be spoken for rejects "any simplistic desire to counter discourses of domination by "letting the native speak."[12] However, as she herself has noted in the preface to her translation of Mahasweta Devi's stories that when the subaltern woman "speaks" in order to be heard and gets into the structure of responsible resistance, he or she is in the way of becoming an organic intellectual. Read in the context of Spivak's own theoretical evolution as well as the evolution of current postcolonial, feminist interventions, the subaltern woman's passage into the realm of intellectuality is important.

For my purpose the issue of women's' voices condensed in the question "Can the Subaltern speak?", specifically in relation to the work of Pratibha Parmar is an important step forward in the theorizing of women's agency and voice-consciousness. However, rather than treat Spivak's statement regarding the female subaltern in "Can the Subaltern Speak?" as an absolute conclusion, I would like to follow the subaltern's progression into the realm of intellectuality and propose (by way of Parmar's work) that subaltern women have opened up spaces for responsible resistance and collective action. And that in the *effectiveness* of their testimonial work I look for strategies of decolonization.

*   *   *

"To be an artist, a lesbian and a woman of color engaged in mapping out our visual imaginations is both exciting and exhausting" writes Pratibha Parmar.[13] The creative upsurge in cultural production and activism by men and women of color in Britain has never received the attention it deserves. And this cannot be attributed to mere oversight. I think it has much more to do with erasing difference and the preservation of an idea or essence of Britishness and British culture that cannot come to terms with the presence of diasporan identities:

> We have been changing the very heart of what constitutes Englishness by recording
> it with our diasporan sensibilities. Our ancestral as well as personal experiences of
> migration, dispersal, and dislocation give us an acute sense of the limitations of
> national identities. Some of us claim an English as well as British identity, and in so
> doing transform the very terrain of Englishness and expose the ruptures in the
> discourses of white supremacy. The fact that British national culture is
> heterogeneous and ethnically differentiated is something that still needs hammering
> home to those who are persistent in their view that to be black and British is an
> anachronism. Our visual outpourings are our referents for our "imagined
> communities" and our utopian visions, which we seek to articulate and live and
> work towards.[14]

There is a particular fusion between aestheticism and activism that informs the theoretical and thematic concerns of Parmar's work. Parmar's films and videos do not speak from a position of marginalization but from resistance to that marginalization. By continuously negotiating the borderlines between shifting territories of margin and center, inclusion and exclusion, visibility and invisibility, Parmar is not interested in defining herself in relation to something or someone else. She is interested in creating a place for herself within different and sometimes contradictory communities, not in relation to, or in opposition to, or reversal of, or correction of something, but in and for herself. Parmar's videos create images of marginalized women, gays, and lesbians of color that enable them to construct their own complexities. Parmar documents and celebrates the stories of these people by foregrounding the joys, the passions, and the desires that characterize their struggle against racial and sexual oppression. For Parmar pleasure is not expressed sexually, but also in recreation of strong and affirming communities. By making organic links between race and sexuality, Parmar foregrounds experiences of migration and displacement, racial, and sexual harassment to construct a whole new language of audio-visual representation. Parmar's aesthetic practices make it possible to arrive at a new perspective on political identities and imagined communities through the process of coming together, communifying and bringing together experiences previously lived as individual and private. The creation of collective agency, within marginalized groups to create an agenda around experiences of racism, sexism, and homophobia leads to a recognition that political communities cannot be hermetically sealed from each other, and must struggle together in contradictory relations.

Seen within this context, Parmar's videos can be read as parodies of the documentary format where interviews, voice over narration, and direct testimonies are *fictionalized* to critique the commodification of ethnicity typical in documentary films. Since aesthetics always acts on politics, Parmar's *documentaries in disguise* also address the problem of testimony and translation or the production of meaning, and cultural identity where unmediated access to authentic reality is questioned.

By escaping both, the purely "authentic" and the purely "fictional", Parmar's videos dramatize the tension between these diametrically opposed genres to give "voice" to marginalized groups who have hitherto been exiles in their own history, or glorified as heroes and heroines, or victimized as bystanders of, and spectators to their own oppression.

Parmar's videos provide spaces where diverse fictions of representation and self-representation come together. The result sometimes is a fabric of "excess" where scenes of fantasy, artifice, and uninhibited theatricality gratuitously co-mingle with scenes of direct and factual testimony. But this is characteristic of Parmar's aesthetics—her *masquerade*—her effort to deliberately "cover-up" or mask any impulse to create a transparent and authentic "voice" or relationship between image and text. Part of Parmar's masquerade has been to show how theory can relate intimately to poetry, and how, by allowing the two to coexist "testimony" can be prevented from becoming dogma. By moving in and out of different languages, genres, and aesthetic practices, Parmar's videos contain within them oppositional discourses that challenge, deconstruct, and reformulate each other's underpinnings. By refusing to take itself for granted, Parmar's visual and verbal language is at its most radical. I begin with *Sari Red*.

SARI RED:

> Let's not sit inside our sorrows, let's not describe
> things to death. My orientation is activism. Other than
> that it's like a kind of vanity or decadence. I will tell
> you how I suffer and you tell me how you suffer . . . it's
> bad enough to suffer but to talk about it endlessly . . . I
> say to them stop it . . . .stop it . . . .[15]

> The women's movement in Britain has never taken up the question of racism in any real way and because this issue effects all black women, we feel that a failure to take it up has ensured and will continue to ensure that the woman's Liberation Movement as a whole is irrelevant to the needs and demands of most black women. It is fairly clear that we are not 'all sisters together' and it is important to understand why this is so. The failure to take this issue seriously has produced certain anomalies in the relationship of feminism to black women and their specific situations.[16]

Sari Red, an eleven-minute video about the killing of a young Asian woman, Kalbinder Kaur Hayre, by white fascists in Dartford, England is one of Parmar's earliest videos. Released in 1988, this video was made and funded almost completely by Parmar. Using a video 8 camera, Parmar creates a strikingly powerful visual poem not just about racism against women, but about the positive, affirmative aspects of being Asian women. She does this by creating representations that challenge the invisibility and stereotypical images of Asian women as meek, passive and submissive, by allowing the testimony of women as victims to turn into an affirmation of women as survivors.

Sari Red explores the experiences of migration, rupture, and struggle within the confines of a racist economy. In this video, Parmar, uses culturally specific (Indian) icons and motifs, not only to give her video and re-presentation of Asian women a particular kind of cultural resonance, but also a certain kind of dissonance that makes it difficult for one to gain easy access to their authenticity.[17] Parmar writes:

> As Asian women we have to place ourselves in the role of subjects creatively engaged in constructing our own images based both in our material and social

conditions. The task of reconstituting the prevailing images of Asian women entails us in a struggle on several fronts. We have to begin by rescuing ourselves and our history from the colonial interpretations which have continued to dehumanize us and belittle us, and recast Asian women as active agents in the making of our history. We have to begin to rescue the strands and threads of past and present experiences and future hopes into a tapestry whose hues and patterns will reflect us in our complexities and our contradictions . . . [18]

So, what you see in *Sari Red* are the daily activities of immigrant women's lives, nothing "exotic", nothing that constitutes the usual focal points of documentary's fetishistic approach to "alien" cultures. However, this rhythm of ordinariness is broken by interspersed images of racial violence.

Critics have pointed out that Parmar works within the boundaries of documentary praxis. By presenting the reality of racial conflict in contemporary British society, Parmar uses documentary's off-screen, invisible narrator to tell the story of one Asian woman's tragic demise in the hands of racist hooligans. Yet, *Sari Red* cannot be understood as a documentary in any classic sense. Nor can it be referred to solely as a commentary or critique of the documentary genre. It can be read as a transformed documentary, or a documentary in disguise, a theoretical/poetic text that *masquerades* as documentary but re-presents the genre by giving its female protagonist a "voice."

Parmar's text is a scholarly text that introduces the mutual challenge of poetry and theory, discursive and non-discursive languages into the parameters of documentary filmmaking. *Sari Red* comes close to the conventions of documentary, as the narrative of the off-screen voice is woven into the fabric of the filmic text with footage of real-life events. However, "every representation of truth involves elements of fiction, and the difference between the so-called documentary mode and fiction in their depiction of reality is perhaps only a question of the degree of fictitiousness. The more one tries to clarify the line dividing the two, the deeper one gets entangled in the artifice of boundaries" (*Framer*, 145).

This is precisely the masquerade of Parmar's video. Rather than create an oppositional discourse, it moves in and out of several discursive modes, reformulating their suppositions and ideological underpinnings. Part of Parmar's strategy is to display how intimately poetry can masquerade as theory and activism and vice-versa. Trinh Minh-Ha comments on the intermingling of poetry and theory in an interview with Pratibha Parmar:

Theorists tend to react strongly against poetry today because for them, poetry is nothing else but a place where subjectivity is consolidated and where language is estheticized. Whereas poetry is also the place from which many people of color voice their struggle . . . So poetic language does become stale and self-indulgent when it serves an art-for-art's sake purpose, but it can also be the site where language is at its most radical in its refusal to take itself for granted.[19]

I will now attempt a reading of Parmar's video as a theoretical/poetical masquerade of conventional documentary practice and suggest that the oral testimony of the voice-over narrator (s) is poeticized, pluralized, and politicized by the "fictions" of documentary. In *Sari Red*, Asian women project themselves through their own stories and resistances by using a repertoire of icons, images, and narrative manipulations to re-enact or stage the horror and anguish of their condition.

Parmar is able to give these women a voice without it being the "authentic," transcendental voice of documentary films. The play on the fictions of documentary is carried out in multiple ways in Parmar's video, but I am particularly interested in the tension between Parmar's "voice-over" narrations and her strategic inclusion of diverse, often contradictory images in the film. This is an extremely effective narrational technique employed by Parmar in her effort to do something other than mirror dominant documentary discourse.

I want to suggest, then, that *Sari Red* is not only a visual montage but an example of narrational montage where the illusion of monologic, synchronized sound and voice cherished by documentarians is continuously disrupted by the filmmaker's manipulations—her play on factualism and authenticity. The same applies to Parmar's use of music, which is not functional or cosmetic, but is used to disrupt continuity, to disorient, to shatter the rhythm of images in such a way that the rhythm of sound in the background is out of sync with the image on the screen. This results in some very ambivalent and disquieting moments.

However, the burden of representation for Parmar in the case of *Sari Red* was to give voice to a subject that has never spoken, without it turning into the transparent voice of authenticity. This is a huge burden and Parmar approaches this problem by shifting her focus from using film merely as an art form, to film as a vehicle to tell, re-tell, or un-tell stories of oppression in a manner that is peculiarly "feminized". This way the work "doesn't announce its agenda, it is not confrontational in the usual sense, and it does not take an overt position in relation to power as it is currently constituted" (*Framer*, 246). But, it employs a structure that is able to permit the contradictory and conflicting temporalities that women are brought into as a result of migration— women as victims of migration, women as survivors and resistors of violence.

Sari Red can also be read as an attempt to represent the role/position of women in the processes of migration and displacement and in the struggle against racism. Parmar writes:

> The emphasis we place on locating racially constructed gender roles within the broader structures of society should not be taken to mean that we see Asian women as being at the mercy of these relations. It is also important to look seriously at the resistance and struggles Asian women have participated in . . . Despite the force of racial stereotypes Asian women do not experience the racism from which they suffer in a passive way. They have developed their own forms of resistance, articulate their own ideas about British society, and rely on their own historical cultural traditions as a means of support. [20]

What you see in *Sari Red* is a very subjective attempt to decolonize media images of Asian women, and although the film speaks of the violation of one particular woman—Kalbinder Kaur Hayre, it does not succumb to the representation of a single self. Parmar is not interested in using media to "express herself," but rather to expose the collective struggle of women. This she does by adopting a plurality of voices and tones under the guise of a single, omniscient narrator.

Sari Red operates like a poetical score that uses poetical language and exotic iconography, not merely as aestheticizing motifs to establish a "subjective" self, but to provide a range of accents and discursive modes. Both sonically and visually, these modes are less pluralizing and more violent in their effects, forcing the viewer to invent a new way of understanding women's oppression and resistance.

In Parmar's film three different narrational voices interact. However, the distinction made by the voices is not a rigid one because they occasionally overlap and co-exist stereophonically; one in the foreground, one in the background, giving the effect of simultaneity and echo—but never in opposition to each other. The film begins with a series of quickly cut, short scenes that give the effect of disjunction between sound and image:

1. Tranquil image of a red sari blowing in the wind against the background of swaying trees. Slow, ominous music shatters the tranquility of the image.
2. Cut to a shot of red blood slowly splattering a brick wall.

3. A series of quick cuts depicting powerful female Indian deities, that could be Kali or different avatars of Kali.[21]
4. Impressionistic shot of a sacrificial altar with burning candles and dark eyes shot in a diffusion of bright colors and lighting effects that give a surrealistic impression of power, potency, and vengeance.
5. Fade to a superimposed shot of a burning Union Jack against the blurred background of exotic and erotic icons.
6. Close up of heavily made-up eyes of a dancer, resembling the "watchful eyes" in the altar shot.
7. Shot of a woman's dancing feet. Apparently the woman is dancing on pieces of glass. There are patches of blood everywhere. This is reminiscent of the shots of dancing women in mainstream, Bollywood Hindi films.
8. The omniscient narration begins:

> *Death against the wall*
> *Blood on the street*
> *Staining, flowing,*
> *Cannot be erased, must not*
> *be erased . . .*

The rhythm and pace of Parmar's poetic film is established in these first scenes which use a great deal of repetition of sounds and images in changing contexts in a way that the spectator has to make the connections between them. Trinh Minh-Ha's reflections on their use in film can be adequately applied to Parmar's strategy in *Sari Red* where repetition ". . . used in the spoken text, for example (fragments of sentences), are never identical. It suffices to pull one out of the repeated sentence to shift its meaning " (*Framer*, 228). Trinh-Minh-Ha continues to describe the effect of repetition in unsettling meaning:

As viewers, we often fix a meaning or metaphor by identifying or associating the image with the commentary that accompanies it. Repetitions of the same sentence (or image) in slightly different forms and in ever-changing contexts help to unsettle such a fixity, and to perceive the plural, sliding relationship between ear and eye, image and word. In instances where repetition functions as a substitute for lengthy scientific—humanistic explanations, it leaves room for the spectator to decide what to make out of the statement or sequences of images in its diversely repeated forms.[22]

Parmar's approach is one that constantly defies the sureness of signification and narration. For example, in the opening section of the film she uses the voice of poetry where factual information (the violation of an Indian woman by three white male fascists) is rendered through repetition and a highly pronounced visual language. The abundance of visual images, the expropriation and appropriation of culturally specific icons, the use of vivid and potent colors, manipulation of light effects, challenge the use of news footage because they defy a systematic reconstruction of linear time by reaching out to the endless possibilities of a dynamic heritage. For instance, Parmar's use of the sari motif (there are long shots of women wearing saris, or shots of different, beautifully patterned saris blowing in the wind), has the effect of disjunction. This happens because never before has a sari—symbol of Indian femininity, sexuality, tradition, and adornment, been used in a film about racial violence. In some ways, the recurrent metaphor of the sari in *Sari Red* suggests the contradictory temporalities that women are brought into through processes of migration and the realities of racism. In Parmar's film, woman as figure of modernity in flux is explored. The sari is the symbol of her journey into (post) modernity, her fragmented entrance into the diaspora, the jarring of where she has come from, and where she is now. The use of powerful feminine images and the stylized rendition of her poetic narrator make it possible for Parmar to give public voice to private emotions without surrendering the specificity and collectivity of women's resistances.

In the second part of her video the narrational voice changes into the discursive voice of a news reporter giving factual information, the names, dates, events, and outcome of the episode of racial violence. The apparent imitation of documentary practice is undermined by the contradiction between voice and image. Elaborate shots of Indian women going about their peaceful, uneventful day to day lives, kneading dough, working in the garden, doing their daily chores is interrupted by the narrated story of Kalbinder Kaur and the ritualistic and repetitive chanting of "Paki wog, Paki wog." This is interspersed by a third narrative voice of poetry creating an effect of polyphony and disruption. So we have in Parmar's film the co-presence of multiple narrational renditions:

Voice # 1: A factual rendition of racial violence.
Voice # 2: A poetic rendition of Kalbinder's resistance, and the attempt by Asian
          women to fight back.
Voice # 3: Ritualistic chanting of "Paki wog."

Sari Red operates more like a musical score than a straightforward documentary film where the horror of racial violence is explored through the poetic language of repetition and metaphor. Both function as transforming and rhythmic structural devices in the text. There is no unifying voice-over and no single voice is given the position of mastery, explanation, or resolution. Also, erratic and often visibly unstable camera movements mark the film. This, combined with the inclusion of similar shots and images photographed from different distances and camera angels and the numerous jump-cuts remind us of the performative and dialogic quality of *Sari Red*. This is also the film's masquerade asserting that no "reality" can be captured without transforming it.

In conclusion: a word about Parmar's attempt to situate women's resistance within the history of migration. By including painted or reproduced pictures and posters of Asian women resistors, the Southall Black Sisters and the Sari Squad in conjunction with potent images of feminine power, Parmar is able to effectively dismantle mainstream notions about passive Asian women propagated by a colonized media. In *Sari Red*, she has been able to situate the forgotten women in the history of diasporic struggles against racism. By giving her protagonist a voice (s), Parmar has rendered the ultimate senselessness and ineffectuality of white male violence. The image of the three male puppets, inanimate and impotent, is reflected against the angry voices of Kalbinder, the narrators, the Southall Black Sisters and the Sari Squad for:

> Angry at this violation she shouted back . . . For her self-respect she shouted back . . . For such violation in public she shouted back . . . Yes she shouted back. Indeed she shouted back. Of course she shouted back.

KHUSH:

With *Khush*[23] Parmar challenges white hegemonic practice by creating a mixture of documentary and art-film savvy to create a work about the lives of South Asian gays and lesbians in India, Britain, and Canada. Despite the double bind of racism and homophobia in their own societies, for the gay and lesbian men and women in Parmar's film, there is an uninhibited affirmation of sexual solidarity and pleasure combined with the oral testimonies of individual experiences of "coming out" and the collective experiences of racism, sexism, colonialism and classism.

Sensual dance, music, and performance vignettes are interspersed with the interviews creating a film that is aesthetically beautiful and erotic. *Khush* is a mixture of documentary realism, lyricism, art and commentary, as well as an important lesson in social history. It attempts to situate homosexuality (commonly believed to be a purely western phenomenon) within the context of ancient Indian history, art, and culture—a complex and rich heritage that was either destroyed or effaced under the prudery of colonial rule to give way to the so-called morality of the West.

Khush was produced in 1991 for Channel 4's *Out on Tuesday,* series. *Out on Tuesday,* commissioned by Caroline Spry is the only lesbian and gay magazine program on Channel 4 that broadcasts independent, alternative documentaries that examine the different aspects of lesbian and gay experiences, both in England and internationally. However, in order to understand this, particularly in a climate where section 28, an anti-lesbian and gay act was passed through parliament, and because of the crisis around AIDS that compounded the already existing prejudice; it seems necessary to focus on the role and potential of activism in Parmar's work.

Khush is, in part, Parmar's filmic answer to the long isolation she experienced as a South Asian lesbian and feminist. Filmed partly in India where homosexuality is illegal, without official permission and often under extremely difficult conditions, Parmar was able to find men and women willing to take the risk to talk specifically about South Asian homosexual issues. These men and women agreed to do this because they believed that if some of them didn't begin to come out, they would never gain visibility as a community.

Khush is a film about promoting communities and potential alliances that could communicate and collaborate across boundaries in order to challenge and activate against forms of domination. It is about gaining strength from the knowledge that these collaborations deepen different, often conflictual locations and histories to develop a global perspective.

For Parmar, transgressive sexual preference is not only about alternate lifestyles but about creating links between personal and political practice, where making alliances is also about listening to other people's perspectives, and alternative television enabled Parmar to gain access to, and organize wider audiences. By providing a space and platform for alternative films, independent queer filmmaking and activism have been able to interrogate and challenge the tired tropes that constitute official versions of history.[24] Kobena Mercer writes:

> Through political activism and new forms of cultural practice, we have created a community that has inspired a new sense of collective identity among lesbian and gay men across the black diaspora . . . It was through the process of coming together—communifying, as it were, that we transformed experiences previously lived as individual, privatized, and even pathologized problems into the basis for a sense of collective agency. This sense of agency enabled us to formulate an agenda

around our experiences of racism in the white gay community and issues of homophobia in black communities to which we equally belong . . . What follows from this is a recognition of the interdependence of different political communities, not completely closed off from each other . . . but interlocking in contradictory relations over which we struggle.[25]

I now begin a reading of *Khush* by suggesting that the film's masquerade lies in its "performative mode" or an acting out and transformation, not imitation, of the repertoire of pleasures produced within mainstream, consumer cultural practices, and therefore a form of resistance. By re-creating and re-enacting situations, which the spectator can identify with in different and contradictory contexts, *Khush*, like *Sari Red*, uses specifically feminine and uniquely South Asian motifs to simulate or dramatize the complexities of gay and lesbian identities. By mixing together, contrasting images and styles in the process of its masquerade, Parmar's film resembles a stylized, artificial rendition of glamorous images that makes possible a reading that contradicts its deeply politicized and radical subject matter.

By appropriating the interview format of conventional documentary films, *Khush* destabilizes the boundaries between 'truth' and artifice, fantasy and reality. The recurrent presence of the 'miming figure' with its painted face and elaborate body movements draws attention to the film's performative quality. Always appearing in the interstices of the 'realistic' interview shots and the non-natural, fantasy segments, this figure is both mimer and mocker of convention. By dissolving the line between fantasy and reality, the self-consciousness of the actors, and the seeming naturalness of the interviewees, it breaks and mocks the secure vision of the voyeur by introducing another version of reality. He is the masquerader that explores the gap between identity and fantasy by bringing erotic ambiguity into the film. He tests our threshold of pleasure and manages to parody and break down dominant patterns of filming pleasure rather than hopelessly imitating it. It gives the film a critical dimension so that it does not come across as a simplistic commodification of ethnicity. It seems to me, though, that the primary task of the mimer is to mock conventions; filmic, sexual, and socio-historic. If one marks the specific moments when he punctuates the film, we notice a significant pattern. He first appears at the beginning of the film:

1. Close-up of dancing feet in a disco.
2. Cut to a shot of the miner dancing in slow motion.

3. Cut to shots of feminine adornments—patterned fabric swaying in the wind, a display of colorful bangles.
4. Cut to the mimer dancing.
5. Slow pan of Indian temples.
6. Mimer dancing.
7. Fade-out of mimer and slow fade-in of the interviewee.

In his first appearance, the mimer dressed like a leopard stealthily dances in mock imitation of the dancers in the disco. Later he ushers in the shots of the temples in slow, erotically lingering movements to signal the appearance of the gay male interviewee discussing the erotic energy latent in Indian art and architecture.

Functioning more or less like a chorus in ancient Greek drama, the miming figure or the figure of masquerade in Parmar's film also functions as a didactic figure. However, didacticism in *Khush* , like in Hanif Kureishi's *Sammy and Rosie Get Laid*, is not based on the old-fashioned, simplistic morality and prudery imposed by the colonial powers. It is interested, rather, in staging the general crisis of the legacy of colonialism and heterosexism. Notice that when the figure reappears, it interrupts the interviewee talking about the destruction and banning of the erotic Khajurao temples by the British, in order to eradicate the heritage and energy of Indian art and impose a false, colonial version of prudery. His presence is therefore both functional and cosmetic:

1. Gay man talking about the banning and destruction of Khajurao by the British.
2. Cut to the mimer.
3. Shots of Indian temples standing solid and indestructible.

In another sequence the mimer stages the prudery of conventional and sexist heterosexual love by signaling the juxtaposition of black and white sequences of dancing women taken from mainstream Hindi films. While this frames the background, in the foreground we see a still shot of two daringly sensuous and beautifully adorned lesbian lovers powerfully undercutting the obvious fetishization and spectacularization of the dancing women in the background.

The recurring premise of Parmar's work has been to create a visual language or aesthetics best suited to her thematic concerns. Originally trained as a researcher in mainstream media, working in documentary films which utilized the conventions of journalism and current affairs, Parmar started to do her own work either through small grants or personal funds. Working with feminist publishers, as a lecturer in a Women's Studies department, and as a youth worker with young Asian women,

Parmar experimented with film technology without any formal training. Many of the metaphors in her films come from her own multiple identities and experiences. In *Khush* the diversity of cultural and racial identities is expressed under the umbrella category of gay and lesbian. However, within this all-encompassing category, Parmar seeks to explore a much broader filmic and political discourse, which is mindful of the multiple locations, geographically, and aesthetically, that gays and lesbians of color occupy.

Parmar's filmic discourse is self-referencing and challenges the Eurocentric and ethnocentric modes of visual and cultural representation by exploring visual languages that attempt to capture the experiences of migration, rupture, and struggle to live within multiple locations, and to sustain multiple strategies of resistance. Using the architectural signs and symbols of 'erotic India,' juxtaposed against contemporary, exploitative, Hindi films; young South Asian gays and lesbians celebrate desire and self-pride through dance, music, and adornment. In *Khush* the dominant motifs of traditional feminine adornment like glass bangles, 'mehndi' (henna applied on hands and feet of Indian brides or temple dancers), indicate beauty, diversity, and a rich cultural heritage that is usually not associated with gay and lesbian identities.

Parmar's aesthetic campaign takes conventional images of passivity, tradition, vulnerability, and exploitation out of their immediate contexts to give them power and versatility. *Khush* is partly an exploration of aesthetic pleasure, part history lesson and part call to action. The film's rhythmic pulse is heightened by the creative linking of the 'interview sections' with the 'aesthetic sections' by the figure of the masquerader. This figure either reinforces each interviewee's account or undercuts it with seemingly gratuitous shots of beautiful women dressed in colorful and erotic costumes, or shots of temple art, images from the *Kama Sutra*, or stills of colorful and visually appealing images of feminine clothing and jewelry.

The entire film is a lyrical and ecstatic conglomeration of images. Yet the dream-like fantasy sequences in the film are interrupted by real-life experiences of gay and lesbian men and women who have been the unjust targets of racism and homophobia. In *Khush,* the bold celebration of gay and lesbian desire undercuts the images used by the West to undermine the political confidence of such marginalized groups. At the same time it challenges the homophobia of South Asian societies by exploring historical constructions of gaity in Indian art and history. Homosexuality is projected not as the bad consequence of migration, but a rich and vibrant part of Indian culture.

In *Kush* , it seems to me, Parmar attempts to challenge the position of "knowledge" as it is derived from documentaries by working with elements of visual fascination and pleasure. "Looking," in Parmar's video induces a different form of spectatorship than one that expects access to knowledge or voyeurism. *Khush* works to forge a connection between the staged and the real—the fictions of film caught in the fictions of life.

The interviews at the beginning of the film are quite consciously and deliberately staged by the way they are conducted, in the studio, with artificial props and lighting. Other interviews are set in natural environments. In the Indian segment of the video, Parmar deliberately uses outdoor settings to give her interviewees a specific location and history. So there are different entries into the film whereby the real and the staged interviews call attention to the politics of interviewing itself. The editing in the 'natural' interview sections is more conventional, with slower, longer sequences shot in natural lighting as the camera pans across crowded streets in India, capturing the sights, sounds and 'normalcy' of daily life. The stylized sections of the video is characterized by a montage of quickly edited shots of men and women talking in studio settings, that draw attention to the illusion of unmediated reality.

By juxtaposing the real and staged interviews, Parmar gives voice to the marginalized subject or the subaltern without it being an "authentic" voice. *Khush* is a video where diverse fictions of representation and self-representation come together, because:

> . . . Interviews which occupy a dominant role in documentary practices-in terms of authenticating information; validating the voices recruited for the sake of the argument of the film advances (claiming however to "give voice" to the people); and legitimizing an exclusionary system of representation based on the dominant ideology of presence and authenticity—are actually sophisticated devices of fiction.[26]

Since speech is tactical, the unveiling of the fictionality of both the staged interviews and the "real interviews" cannot be considered as representing "truth." Parmar intersperses the two in order to question unmediated access to authentic reality via the interview, by setting the stage to solicit the viewer's critical ability before the "real" interviews are introduced. However, the so—called spontaneous words of a woman sitting against the background of ancient monuments in Delhi, or the man talking about sexuality, classism, and the inability of middle class morality to accept gayness, or of the man in his neighborhood who talks about the persecution and dangers of coming out, or of the gay male discussing the strength of networking and providing valuable information about existing gay and lesbian groups in Britain, India, and Canada, are no less staged than the reenacted ones. But now the staging is masked, concealed, hidden, because it is no longer obviously perceptible via the mise-en-scene, but via situating, framing, editing, and contextualizing. The film, then, begins by calling attention to its staged quality by providing a rich amalgamation of isolated and superimposed images of clothing, jewelry, and other "exotica" against a musical score that is varied in its modes—sensuous, rhythmic, and celebratory. The video then moves on to contrast this with representations of "realistic" or unstaged glimpses into the lives and activities of gay men and women.

* * *

The recurring emphasis in Parmar's work has been on the exploration of self-affirmation that's come out of the cultural and political struggles initiated by marginalized individuals and communities. Both *Sari Red* and *Emergence*,[27] make strong statements that if one is able to articulate one's situation as a victim then one can become a survivor.

But Parmar is not just concerned with "giving voice" to women and other oppressed groups to empower them, because the notion of "giving voice" itself is charged with the implication that you have to be in a controlling position to "give voice" to other people. No matter how plural or diverse the voices featured in Parmar's film, one has to point back to the apparatus and site from which these voices are brought together. The notion of voice remains paternalistic, and although Spivak cautions us in her essay about the dangers of attempting to extricate a voice of authenticity, the voice of truth; she confines her argument to the idea that one has to think about extracting a subaltern voice *on its own terms*. Moreover the notion of empowering the disenfranchised through speech is problematic, because women's relationship to language itself is uncomfortable, particularly since language can never be neutral. Trinh-Minh-Ha points out that ". . . it is the site where power relations are most complex and pernicious; yet it is also a place of liberation. Whether it frees or enslaves depends on how it is used, and it is pernicious only when its workings are invisible. So having the women articulate their oppression is not enough. One has to do something to point to both the fact that language is a *tool* of power and the fact that possessing power is like owning a leaking boat . . ." (*Framer*, 160–170).

Spivak's question "Can the Subaltern Speak?", then, is better rephrased as "In what ways does the subaltern speak?". Parmar's videos answer this by re-enacting the multifaceted nature of cultural formation, the diasporic experience of colonization, domination, exclusion, and fragmentation by searching for a *form* to articulate marginal experiences. Embracing, in some ways, the legacy of intellectualism inherited by them from their oppressors, black artists of the new generation have had to move between the cultures and languages of domination in order to search for a vocabulary that does not victimize or oppress but transforms the language of media colonization, or even the language of academia to mobilize lived experiences and resistances.[28] And this is the ultimate task of Parmar's masquerade—to bring into being new and conflictual critiques of visual and verbal languages by making the crisis that underlies the notion of voice, testimony, narration, language speak.

I would like to conclude by quoting from Algerian feminist/writer/activist Assia Djebar's novel *Fantasia: An Algerian Cavalcade* where Djebar reflects on just such a crisis, and the burden of her own westernized, and intellectualized heritage. This she presents through her conflict between using her mother tongue, Arabic versus her adopted language of migration—French. In this section titled *Soliloquy*, she writes:

> *My fiction is this attempt at biography, weighed down under the oppressive burden of my heritage. Shall I sink beneath the weight? . . . But the tribal legend criss-crosses the empty spaces, and the imagination crouches in the silence when loving words of the un-written mother-tongue remain unspoken—language conveyed like the babbling of a nameless, haggard murmur—crouches in this dark night like a woman begging in the streets . . . I shelter again in the shade of my cloistered companions' whispers. How shall I find the strength to tear off my veil, unless I have to use it to bandage the running sore nearby from which words exude?*[29]

The healing potential of Djebar's veil, or mask, or masquerade reiterates the point that I am making, that it is important to ask not if the subaltern can speak or if it is possible for the subaltern to find the strength to tear off the veil of isolation and oppression. It is important to ask in what way it is possible to use that veil to unmask the dilemmas of language and voice to aid and empower the subaltern to find a voice. Rephrasing the question in this way enables us to retain Spivak's insights about the peculiar positioning of the subaltern in colonial discourse without undermining the possibilities of creating *new* and dynamic spaces without conceding to, in the words of Lata Mani, ". . . colonial discourse what it, in fact, did not (*and cannot*) achieve . . ." (*Cultural*, 403);—the erasure of subalternity.

Figure 3. Pratibha Parmar, *Sari Red*

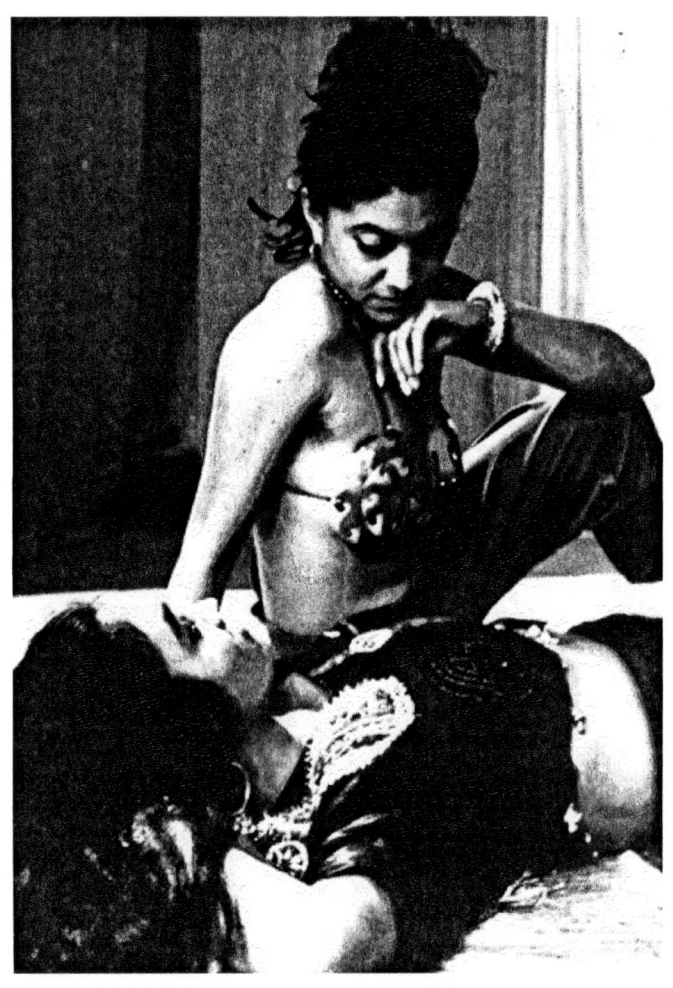

Figure 4. Pratibha Parmar, *Khush*

NOTES

1. Gayatri Chakravorty Spivak, "Can the Subaltern Speak?", *Marxism and the Interpretation of Culture*, Cary Nelson and Lawrence Grossberg, eds. (Chicago: U of Illinois P, 1988) 297.

2. I use the word "subaltern" loosely. It was first used by Antonio Gramsci to mean low ranking officer in the British colonial army in India, himself a native disciplined by the British to rule unruly natives. Subsequently, the term was borrowed by the Subaltern Studies Group that proposed to rewrite Indian history from the perspective of the subaltern. However, now it has been applied to any non-elite, oppressed or marginalized subjects, including women, and has, on occasion, lost its class specific usage. However, it has retained its colonial connotations to include tribal women or colonized women. The word "subaltern" has, therefore, lost both political and intellectual connotations and for my purposes, I draw freely on both.. See Ranajit Guha and Gayatri Chakravorty Spivak, eds. *Selected Subaltern Studies* (New York: Oxford UP, 1988), Gayatri Chakravorty Spivak, *In Other Worlds: Essays in Cultural Politics* (New York and London: Routledge, 1988). The idea of the subaltern woman as organic intellectual, however, has been proposed by Gayatri Spivak in her discussion of writer, Mahasweta Devi's tribal heroines. Originally presented by Gramsci in his *Prison Notebooks*, to signify the homogeneity given to a single social group by a strata of intellectuals, the term "organic intellectual" has been reused by Spivak within an entirely different context— the context of Indian tribal history and literature (particularly the work of Mahasweta Devi) where Spivak points out the primary role of subaltern women to be an active participation in practical life as organizers, insurgents, and activists. In Spivak's usage, as also in mine, the term "organic intellectual" is not so much an elaboration of identity as an emphasis on the subaltern woman activist's role and responsibility as an intellectual. See Gayatri Chakravorty Spivak, *Imaginary Maps: Three Stories by Mahasweta Devi* (New York and London: Routledge, 1995), Antonio Gramsci, *Selections from the Prison Notebooks* (New York: International Publishers, 1991).

3. Hazel Carby and bell hooks have pointed out the impossibility of making any easy parallelisms between the position of the white woman and blacks or other subordinate races. Even though the categories of race and gender are both socially constructed; ultimately the experience of the white woman is quite different from that of other racial minorities. In fact it is a mistake to claim the position of the white woman is like the position of ethnic minorities because both take on the role of the Other in relation with the white man. The danger of substituting the position of white women with other minorities overlooks the position of the minority woman! What is lost in this process of substitution is any attempt to theorize the peculiar oppression of the minority woman. This is probably why Fanon maintained, "I know nothing about her." For more information on the problems of theorizing the position of the

minority woman, see Hazel Carby, "White Woman Listen! Black Feminism and the Boundaries of Sisterhood,"*The Empire Writes Back: Race and Racism in 70's Britain*, Center for Contemporary Cultural Studies (London: Hutchinson, 1982), and bell hooks, *Ain't I a Woman: Black Women and Feminism* (Boston: South End P, 1981). See also Elizabeth Spelman, *Inessential Woman: Problems of Exclusion in Feminist Thought* (Boston: Beacon P, 1988).

    4. Gayatri Chakravorty Spivak, "Can the Subaltern Speak?", *Marxism and the Interpretation of Culture*, Cary Nelson and Lawrence Grossberg, eds. (Chicago: U of Illinois P, 1988) 303.

    5. Gayatri Chakravorty Spivak, "Can the Subaltern Speak?",*Marxism and the Interpretation of Culture*, Cary Nelson and Lawrence Grossberg, eds. (Chicago: U of Illinois P, 1988) 307.

    6. Gayatri Chakravorty Spivak, "Can the Subaltern Speak?"*Marxism and the Interpretation of Culture*, Cary Nelson and Lawrence Grossberg, eds. (Chicago: U of Illinois P, 1988) 307.

    7. Gayatri Chakravorty Spivak, "Can the Subaltern Speak?",*Marxism and the Interpretation of Culture*, Cary Nelson and Lawrence Grossberg, eds.(Chicago: U of Illinois P, 1988) 307-308.

    8. Gayatri Chakravorty Spivak, *Imaginary Maps: Three Stories by Mahasweta Devi* (New York and London: Routledge, 1995) 17-18.

    9. Gayatri Chakravorty Spivak, *Imaginary Maps: Three Stories by Mahasweta Devi* (New York and London: Routledge, 1995) 25.

    10. Jaladhar Sabar is a member of the "Sabar" tribe in West Bengal. For more information on Sabar's role as an "organic intellectual," see Gayatri Chakravorty Spivak, *Imaginary Maps: Three Stories by Mahasweta Devi* (New York and London: Routledge, 1995) 209.

    11. Gayatri Spivak herself acknowledges the difference between the need for the subaltern to "speak" in order to be heard rather than be spoken for, in her translation of Mahasweta Devi's stories. This crucial difference is remarkably absent or unacknowledged in her essay "Can the Subaltern Speak?". See Gayatri Chakravorty Spivak, *Imaginary Maps: Three Stories by Mahasweta Devi* (New York and London: Routledge, 1995) 26.

    12. Lata Mani, "Cultural Theory, Colonial Texts: Reading Eyewitness Accounts of Widow Burning," *Cultural Studies*, Lawrence Grossberg, Cary Nelson, Paula Treichler, eds. (New York and London: Routledge, 1992) 396.

    13. Pratibha Parmar, "The Moment of Emergence, " *Queer Looks: Perspectives on Lesbian and Gay Film and Video*, Martha Gever. John Greyson, Pratibha Parmar, eds. (New York and London: Routledge, 1993) 3.

14. Pratibha Parmar, "The Moment of Emergence," *Queer Looks: Perspectives on Lesbian and Gay Film and Video*, Martha Gever, John Greyson, Pratibha Parmar, eds. (New York and London: Routledge, 1993) 3–4.

15. Pratibha Parmar, "Other Kinds of Dreams: An Interview with June Jordan," *Feminist Review* 31 (1989): 62.

16. Pratibha Parmar, "Other Kinds of Dreams: An Interview with June Jordan," *Feminist Review* 31 (1989): 56.

17. One critic from San Francisco complained that **Sari Red** was a 'closed text', and found it difficult to access it, because it did not have any universal resonance. Parmar's response: "I have quite deliberately used Indian icons, Indian motifs which have a particular kind of resonance . . . I don't feel I want to compromise my own visual language in order to make it of 'universal' significance . . . And in a way it's what we as feminists and lesbians have said about a whole number of areas we have been involved in culturally . . . .—that if people can't find easy access into what we are trying to say, well, *they're* going to have to do the work."

18. Pratibha Parmar, "Hateful Contraries: Media Images of Asian Women," *Ten-8* 16, (1984): 78.

19. Trinh Minh-Ha, *Framer Framed* (New York and London: Routledge, 1992) 154.

20. Pratibha Parmar, "Gender, Race, and Class: Asian Women in Resistance," Center for Contemporary Cultural Studies, *The Empire Strikes Back: Race and Racism in 70's Britain* (London: Hutchinson, 1982) 239.

21. In Indian mythology the goddess Kali and her different *avatars* or manifestations have always been associated with anger, power, immense potency and destructiveness.

22. Trinh-Minh-Ha, *Framer Framed* (New York and London: Routledge, 1992) 228.

23. *Khush* is the Urdu word for ecstatic pleasure.

24. Opportunities have both expanded and contracted, funding has both increased and decreased for alternative video, and distribution has both mushroomed and dwindled. For an interesting account of British TV's role in promoting alternative filmmaking and encouraging talent from outside the mainstream, its subsequent restructuring, the future of channel 4, the re-regulation and restructuring of independent production, its impact on women and black filmmakers, and the current tension between causalization and unionization. See, Stuart Hood, ed., *Behind the Screens: The Structure of British Television in the Nineties* (London: Lawrence and Wishart, 1994).

25. Martha Gever, John Greyson, Pratibha Parmar, eds. *Queer Looks: Perspectives on Lesbian and Gay Film and Video* (New York and London: Routledge, 1993) 238–239.

26. Trinh Minh-Ha, *Framer Framed* (New York and London: Routledge, 1992) 193.

27. This is a twenty-minute video made by Parmar in 1986 where black and third world women artists and poets speak about their suppression.

28. The black independent film and video sector in England brought with it an immense diversity of individuals and groups involved in film production. Groups and collectives like Ceddo, Black Audio Film Collective, Sankofa, and Retake were formed by individuals that were also intellectuals—all well versed in contemporary cultural theories. Most of these individuals entered television and film by way of personal experiences of marginalization and indebtedness to a growing intellectualism that seemed to have penetrated film and video production.

29. Assia Djebar, *Fantasia: An Algerian Cavalcade* (Portsmouth: Heinemann, 1993) 218–219.

CHAPTER FOUR

Photography as Mask: Edward Said's *After the Last Sky*

These two communities must be seen as equal to each other . . . only from such a beginning can justice then proceed . . . The peace process as now understood is a process with no true peace at all . . . I urge fellow Palestinians, Arabs, Israelis, Europeans and Americans not to flinch from the unpalatable truth and to demand a reckoning from the unscrupulous leaders who have lied about the facts and tampered with the lives of far too many decent people.[1]

In photography, proficiency of execution may also be interpreted as mask or disguise . . . we who prepare to meet the faces that we meet may be convinced that only surprise will catch a glimpse of truth . . . [2]

Postmodern art cannot be political, at least in the sense that its representations—its images and stories—are anything but neutral, however 'aestheticized' they may appear to be in their parodic self-reflexivity. While the postmodern has no effective theory of agency that enables a move into political *action*, it does work to turn its inevitable ideological grounding into a site of de-naturalizing critique.[3]

. . . the only acceptable political logic for Palestinians is to move our struggle from the level of high-ranking negotiations to the level of the actual on-the-ground reality . . . Political separation is at best a makeshift measure. Partition is a legacy of imperialism, as the unhappy cases of Pakistan and India, Ireland, Cyprus, and the Balkans amply testify, and as the disasters of the 20th century Africa attest in the most tragic way. We must now begin to think in terms of co-existence, after separation, in spite of partition. And for this, . . . the only solution is a politics of the local people on the ground who tackle injustice and inequity on the ground, far away from the misleading summits with Clinton.[4]

Identity—who we are, where we come from, what we are—is difficult to maintain
in exile . . . we are the 'other', an opposite, a flaw in the geometry of resettlement,
an exodus. Silence and discretion veil the hurt, slow the body searches, soothe the
sting of loss.[5]

In an increasingly global and migratory world, Edward Said, both cultural theorist
and political spokesperson, locates the 'mask' of identity. For him identity
formation is itself a masquerade that continuously remakes itself . And, the crucial
question for the Palestinians is the problem of working out an identity politics based
on co-existence rather than exclusion.

With the Palestinian-Israeli peace process in jeopardy, Said's interventions
need to be seen as discursive spaces through which the " dying ideology of
separation" that currently informs peace negotiations can be transformed into the
more urgent philosophical problem of how to live with the "other". Said is bitingly
critical of Yasser Arafat's current role as negotiator and believes that the lack of
popular consent that characterizes and defines his methods now are completely
contradictory to the resistance that symbolized his efforts in the past. Arafat's
compromising diplomacy is disabling for the cause of the Palestinian people's
displacement, landlessness, and exile. At the heart of the Palestinian peace process
then, are the disturbing postcolonial questions of identity politics, exile, and
community. Exile is, of course, tied to the notion of homeland and to the possibility
of return.[6] The nature and logistics of this "return", and the configuration of a new
homeland is precisely what preoccupies Said today. However, within this context of
contaminated post-colonial displacements, the possibility of a complete and
unhindered belonging is impossible. Yet, Said believes, it is important for the
disenfranchised Palestinians to give "voice" to their own troubled identities. Within
the context of the current debate and negotiations of a Palestinian peace accord,
then, it becomes urgently necessary to read Palestinian experiences of exile and
dislocation.

Home is not a real place. It is a re-imagination of ephemeral, and transient
memories and feelings. Dislocation, however, is both personal and culturally
specific. It is an endless effort to both mask and unveil the traumas and anguish of
exile. Today, Said points out, the Palestinians "cannot reach the 'interior', *al-
dakhil*, which refers to both historical Palestine, which is controlled by Israel, but
also to privacy, a kind of wall created by the solidarity forged by members of the
group" (*Edward*, 125). However, Said is not arguing, as Ashcroft and Ahluwalia
point out, that there can be no inner life or community for the Palestinian. He
argues that the search for community, solidarity and identity is the inner experience

that the Palestinian is in search of. This predicament of public and private Palestinian lives is unveiled in Edward Said's photographic essay *After the Last Sky: Palestinian Lives*. Read in the context of the current impasse or failure to negotiate a settlement, the book attains a renewed poignancy in its endless attempt to express or narrate not just the separate history of Palestinian suffering, but also the intermeshed co- existence of many histories, many lives.

In this chapter I will continue the discussion of masquerade as a method of subversion and community building through a discussion of Edward Said's book of photographs—*After the Last Sky: Palestinian Lives*[7] to discuss some of the issues surrounding Palestinian exile and identity.

Said's theoretical/personal/political and poetical rendition of complex lives of Palestinians living in exile combined with the photographs of Jean Mohr is a remarkable venture into the arena of postmodernism where different discourses co-exist and intersect to create a plurality of experiences. In Said's book this plurality also serves as a source of communifying the scattered and disenfranchised living of exile. Said, like Parmar brings together disparate peoples (voices) to create a complex and multilayered network of representations that serve to undermine dominant and hegemonic recreations of marginalized and excluded peoples:

> The whole point of this book is to engage this difficulty, to deny the habitually simple, even harmful representations of Palestinians, and to replace them with something more capable of capturing the complex reality of their experience. Its style and method—the interplay of text and photos, the mixture of genres, modes, styles—do not tell a consecutive story, nor do they constitute a political essay. Since the main features of our present existence are dispossession, dispersion, and yet also a kind of power incommensurate with our stateless exile, I believe that essentially unconventional, hybrid, and fragmentary forms of expression should be used to represent us. What I have quite consciously designed, then, is an alternative mode of expression to the one usually encountered in the media, in works of social science, in popular fiction. It is a personal rendering of the Palestinians as a dispersed national community— acting, acted upon, proud, tender, miserable, funny, indomitable, ironic, paranoid, defensive, assertive, attractive, compelling.[8]

Said's book seems to be a hybrid and postmodern representation of Palestinian lives with all the multitudes of experiences that characterize that life. However, Said's attempt at "humanizing" a set of people also carries with it the additional burden of de-naturalizing them by subverting dominant representations of them. And this, I believe, he does through the employment of masquerade or parody whereby both his text and the photographs, not always in harmony with each other, serve to both undermine and emphasize each other by simultaneously masking and revealing the "reality" that lies behind them. As a form of ironic representation, masquerade is doubly coded in political terms; it both legitimizes and resists that which it parodies.

By contextualizing and deconstructing the lives of dispersed people, Said recreates new and multiple ways of seeing Palestinians. By reconnecting them with a history that is specifically their own, Said attempts through his narrative and Mohr's pictures to emphasize a deep rupture with the past as well as offer new possibilities for the future.

Since I have described and characterized Said's methodology to be postmodern, I wish to emphasize that Said's use of photographic masquerade is the central characteristic of his postmodernism. By combining the visual and the verbal, Said's strategy is both double edged and paradoxical in its relation to history and art tradition. It is both critical and complicates that which precedes it. The tension between inscription and subversion, construction and deconstruction in Said's book upsets learned notions of the relations between text/image, realism/artifice, theory/practice by borrowing and incorporating elements from all.

I would like to preface my reading of Said's text, with a discussion of the status of photography as postmodern art. Then, I will move on to discuss Said's narrative by suggesting that Said employs the characteristic component of postmodernism—parody and masquerade to both subvert dominant notions of Palestinian lives and re-create a context for a people that have not only been disenfranchised but also dehistoricized.

PARODIC PRACTICES: PHOTOGRAPHY, POLITICS AND POSTMODERNISM:

Linda Hutcheon has suggested that photography is probably the perfect postmodern vehicle because it is based on a set of paradoxes that are inherent to its medium. I quote her at length:

> Photography could be seen as Baudrillard's perfect industrial simulacrum: it is, by definition, open to copy, to infinite duplication . . . Yet photography has also become high art: that is, singular, authentic, complete with the Benjaminian 'aura.' . . . photographs are also everywhere in mass culture, from advertising and magazines to family vacation snapshots. And its very instrumentality (be it in terms of either documentary testimony or consumerist persuasion) would seem to contest the formalist view of the photograph as autonomous work of art. There are still

other paradoxes at the heart of the photographic medium . . . Postmodern photographic work, in particular, exploits and challenges both the objective and subjective, the technological and the creative.[9]

If the paradoxical nature of photography constitutes its postmodernism, what makes photography subversive? I believe that photography can achieve subversion through masquerade and parody. Because its transparency seems to offer a more direct view to reality than cinema or television, photography can fall into the trap of mimetic representation. However, that sense of the familiar and natural conveyed by photography can also challenge its transhistorical, familiar, and natural image. In Said's text, I believe, photographic representation works at two levels; on the one hand it deliberately tries to familiarize or humanize a race that has always been represented by media as violent terrorists, to make them appear "normal" like snapshots in a family album. And, on the other hand, the text defamiliarizes the apparent normalcy of the photographs. In this lies the political potential of Said's parodic masquerade. The photographic semblance of the eternal, universal, and uncomplicated mass of people point to the coded and constructed nature of all cultural messages.

In *Ideology and the Image*, Bill Nichols points out that the visual image is a mute object and its meaning "though rich, may be profoundly imprecise, ambiguous, even deceiving. The addition of a verbal text to the visual, then, may be viewed as a means of both securing and disrupting meaning. In any case the text never guarantees a single meaning. However, its potential to influence and guide interpretation is consciously problematized in Said's text where the relationship between the pictoral and the verbal only appears to be complementary. Often Said's text does not elaborate or add any extra information directly to the photograph. It works, instead, like the Derridian supplement, which by masking the obvious relationships between the two genres, serves to denaturalize them.

In *After the Last Sky*, the photographs are both parodic and paradoxical. By incorporating elements of documentary realism, Said's text like Parmar's videos unmasks the constructed nature of these elements. Palestinian lives are not so much described or depicted as constructed. They foreground the choices made by the photographer and the narrator who combines them, and meaning is generated in—between or on the fringes of these two modes. It is, therefore, a hybrid representation:

> If photography is, as a visual medium, inherently paradoxical, it is also semiotically hybrid . . . it is both *indexical* (its representation is based on some physical

connection) and *iconic* (it is a representation of likeness) in its relation to the real. This complex hybrid nature is another reason why photography has become particularly important in a time of challenge to modes of representation. Photographic postmodern art contributes yet another complication . . . the addition of language is the addition of the *symbolic* to the *indexical* and the *iconic* . . . [10]

The process of reading the conventions of both the visual and the verbal requires a mediation that is inscribed within two different systems. And this mediation is the process of masquerade that problematizes and de-naturalizes the history and politics of different and multiple forms of representations. Masquerade also has the ability to connect the present to the past without positing the transparency of either visual or verbal representation. Since it is fundamentally critical and ironic and not nostalgic, "postmodern parody is both deconstructively critical and constructively creative, paradoxically making us aware of both the limits and powers of representation—in any medium" (*Politics*, 98). By demonstrating the intertextual nature of production of meaning, masquerade achieves a critical distance from one's deepest commitments and desires. I now turn to the text.

MASQUERADE AND ITS POLITICS:

After the Last Sky is divided into four sections and is an interesting mixture of different modes and genres—personal and political history, fiction, poetry, theory, social text, and photography through which Said re-thinks questions of community, nation, and identity. I attempt to read the photographs in Said's text as transcriptions of the real whereby the photographs themselves become masks— concealing what is behind them and thwarting confrontation with the real. Roland Barthes writes, "since every photograph is contingent . . . Photography cannot signify except by assuming a mask" (73). For my purpose, however, the mask operates in the realm of ambiguous identity.

In the first section, **"States,"** Said presents an existential view of Palestinian life and space. Most of the pictures in this section are static, representing alienated figures in different forms of exile. In these early sections, the subjects wear no masks and appear to have no names, no future, conceal nothing, and barely exist as isolated individuals. Said writes:

> Exile is a series of portraits without names, without contexts. Images that are largely unexplained, nameless, mute. I look at them without precise anecdotal knowledge, but their realistic exactness makes a deeper impression than mere information. [11]

Completely in contrast with Said's assertions about the "realism" of these mute figures is the staged quality of their exile. Parodying the traditions of documentary realism, the photographs of the veiled woman with her child (figure 5) and the man sitting alone in a chair (p. 13 in the book), foreground their own constructed quality through the blatant manipulations of light and dark effects. In both pictures the play of light transfixes the subjects and renders them mute in their position of immobility, recreating the pathos of their situation. Resembling camera stills, the staged or artificial quality of these pictures masquerading as "real", denies easy accessibility and identification with the photographed subjects. In figure 6, however, we have what appears to be a naturalistic photograph of a solitary infant under a tent in a Bedouin encampment near Beersheba. Taken from a high angle, this photograph presents the exile of the nameless, identity—less child as a commodity for the viewer's sympathy. The insignificance, helplessness, and smallness of the innocent and sleeping child in the barren landscape that surrounds him humanizes the pathos of exile, and the strategic placement of the dog contributes to the artifice of the picture. Here, even though there is a distance between the camera and the subject, there is no critical distance between the viewer/reader. The visual effect, however, is not of complicity but of indifference on the part of nature. The extent and distance of the background out of doors seems exaggerated. The background is backdrop. Nature is both removed and awesome, and yet can be made to stand still for a picture in which it will suggest the impersonality and hostility of the natural world. In figure 7, the skeletal form of a scarecrow is made to represent the plight of exile. Here exile is not humanized but symbolized by the image of the scarecrow confined, or imprisoned within the barbed wire fences. But what appears to be the symbol of exile is humanized by the story of Emile Habiby that accompanies it. This gives the scarecrow a potential name, place and history. However, like his identity the stasis of the scarecrow is transformed into mutability by the text that precedes it:

> How rich our mutability, how easily we change (and are changed) from one thing
> to another, how unstable our place-and all because of the missing foundation of
> our existence, the lost ground of our origin, the broken link with our land and our
> past. There are no Palestinians. Who are the Palestinians?[12]

In the space of one page Said, through his verbal and Mohr's visual montage, denies and affirms the identity of exiled Palestinians. As the text proceeds, the stasis gives way to movement. The photograph of the Israeli soldier in the foreground and the Palestinian boy in the background (p. 42 in the book) parodies the depth of film's deep focus shot and crystallizes the relationship between the foreground and the background, the Israeli's and the Palestinians in terms of separation and inside/outside spaces.

While intimate memory and contemporary social reality characterizes the first section, the second section "Interiors" continues Said's preoccupation with space. Now he concentrates on situations of exile within Palestine, and most of the photographs in this section work as supplements to the text because they are presented in terms of inside/outside spaces. Here, Said dwells on aspects of Palestinian home and family life. The compulsion to repeat that characterizes Palestinian lives is projected in the content and composition of the photographs in this section. This repetition characterizes a living continuum of a past and present, and the closeness and clutter of everyday life is portrayed in the pictures.

The photographs parody the banal quality of snapshots in family albums. If we look closely, however, the ritualistic quality of the photographs is undercut by an alienated quality that may not be immediately obvious to the cursory viewer. In figure 8, this is apparent when the blurred, slightly out-of-focus picture of the little boy is subsumed by the clutter of his interior space, both confining and overcoming him. And, in the background is the picture of John F. Kennedy and the American flag indicating the intrusive presence of America within the private space of Palestinian life. The apparently 'normal' picture of the boy is both contextualized and deconstructed by Said's comments on dislocation, confining spaces, and the history of conquests in Palestine.

Said moves on to briefly describe the state of women's disenfranchisement. In this section, history masquerades as personal memory to recount the mediated plight of Palestinian women. He recounts the disappearance of his mother's identity when her passport was ripped apart, to enable the British to "provide a legal place for one more Jewish immigrant" (*After*, 78).

In figure 9, the familiar portrait of Mrs. Farraj is used by Said as a way of connecting his family with his past. Here, Said uses the intimacy of a photograph of an acquaintance to build communities:

> Here is another face of a woman spun out with the familiarity of years, concealing a lifetime of episodes, splendidly recorded by a listening photographer. It is a face, I thought when I first saw it, of our life at home. Six months later I was showing the pictures casually to my sister. 'There's Mrs. Farraj,' she said . . . Connected to me, my sister, my friends, her relatives, her acquaintances, and the places she's been, her picture seems like a map pulling us all together . . . As soon as I recognized Mrs. Farraj, the suggested intimacy of the photograph's surface gave way to an

explicitness with few secrets. She is a real person-Palestinian- with a real history at the interior of ours. But I don't know whether the photograph can, or does, say things as they really are. Something has been lost. But the representation is all we have. [13]

The intimacy of Mrs. Farraj's close-up undermined by the last paragraph of Said's text and the woman in the picture, gives up her status as "real" and assumes the form of a representation—or mask of the real. Mrs. Farraj is both real and a representation, and in her contradictory parodies of reality and representation, her plight resembles that of the Palestinians who are also both real and representations in Said's text. Mrs. Farraj is both revelation and concealment. The notion of mask is always present.

In the final two sections of *After the Last Sky*, **"Emergence,"** and **"Past and Future,"** Said's narrative becomes more factual and abandons the casual storytelling mode of the earlier sections. Also, in these sections the photographs themselves acquire masks. When seen in isolation, they appear to be stripped of personal and historical contexts, and seem to have no names, no past, and no future. When seen in relation with each other and with Said's text, they begin to acquire identities, communities, histories, as well as a past and a future. They now appear as concrete experiences.

These sections, I believe, are truly subversive because they attribute an identity, a context, a complexity and a community consistently denied to an alienated people. Timeless, pastoral scenes of rural women walking are juxtaposed with myriad photographs of scattered Palestinians in their daily lives as workers and laborers. And these photographs that give local color to Palestinian lives intermingle with Said's narration of Palestinian oppression and resistance in terms of a series of complex, difficult, and changing truths about Palestinian lives.

Even though the content of Said's text foregrounds the subjugation and domination of Palestinian people, the photographs, myriad, heterogeneous, and scattered as they are, are concrete representations that talk to each other and give voice to the resistances of an otherwise marginalized community. The disjunction between text and photographs in the final sections give rise to modes of subversion. For instance, Said speaks about the American reaction to militant Palestinian students in the occupied territories, and the impossibility of influencing American students to support the Palestinian cause:

Or take the American reaction to the militant Palestinian students in the Occupied Territories. These students have quite literally become the vanguard of struggle against occupation, but they have paid a steep price in arrests, houses demolished . . . Since that time the situation has worsened considerably. And still it is next to impossible to interest most American intellectuals in joining the effort . . .[14]

Juxtaposed against this background of American non-cooperation is a tranquil picture of two students talking to each other at Bir Zeit. The political indifference of American intellectuals is translated into the positive communication and community building of Palestinians:

I feel that as Palestinians we must have faith in ourselves as a people with important resources of hope. And as Palestinians and Arabs we must remember that our desire to coexist in peace with each other and with our neighbors is sustained not by blind loyalty . . . but by an abiding faith in real justice and self-determination.[15]

In *After the Last Sky* Said negotiates a national space for a suppressed and dispossessed people. And, writing in exile for him is not merely a metaphor for the "postmodern" condition, but an actual experience of the impossibility to return to a community. This brings to Said's work an acutely political engagement. His unmasking of the Palestinians' transparencies in terms of complex and concrete experiences is linked to his perception of the importance of the intellectual's communitarian affiliations as well as the shifting and dialectical positions of different communities. Hence, rather than perform an analysis of Said's critical/cultural/ theoretical writing, I have chosen to explore Said's role as the representative figure of "Palestine", who, as he testifies in his book, is a direct consequence of unjust oppression. As Ella Shohat points out, in Edward Said's case, "academic vocation has not been divorced from political activism" (*Edward*, 121).

* * *

The Palestinian question is a political issue that has long been regarded as explosive. Often described by the media in violent metaphors, the critical discourse that describes the Israeli-Palestinian negotiations in binary terms of self/other *masks* the complex struggle of ordinary Palestinian life. By homogenizing the experiences of dislocation, the 'metaphoric schema' created by dominant discourses (and political peace brokers on both sides) have undermined the vulnerability of the Palestinians and destroyed the possibilities of co-existence. On February 13, yet another deadline to negotiate a framework for peace was missed by Ehud Barak and Yasser Arafat. This may possibly be one of the worst moments in the long and anguished history of negotiations. Furthermore, the brutal repression combined with tactics of intimidation and border control has diminished all prospects of forging a deal that is acceptable to local Palestinians. Amidst these uncertainties, Said attempts, through his cultural and political writing to offer a critical view of both the Israeli and the Palestinian positions. Severely critical of Arafat's own policing mechanism Said believes the *intifadah*, which began as a movement of Palestinian resistance, not terrorism, has now been terminated by the PLO and the plight of the ordinary Palestinians in exile remains unchanged. They continue to harbor hopes for a peace that remains elusive, contingent, a mask. I conclude with Said's words:

> I occasionally experience myself as a cluster of flowing currents. I prefer this to the idea of a solid self, the identity to which so many attach so much significance. These currents with the themes of one's life, flow along during the waking hours, and at their best, they require no reconciling, no harmonizing. They are "off" and may be out of place, but at least they are always in motion, in time, in place, in the form of all kinds of combinations moving about, not necessarily forward, sometimes against each other, contrapuntally yet without one central theme. A form of freedom, I'd like to think, even if I am far from being totally convinced that it is . . . With so many dissonances in my life I have learned actually to prefer being not quite right and out of place.[16]

This is Said's masquerade, his resistance, his way of coping with the confusions and torments of life lived between multiple identities, and cultures.

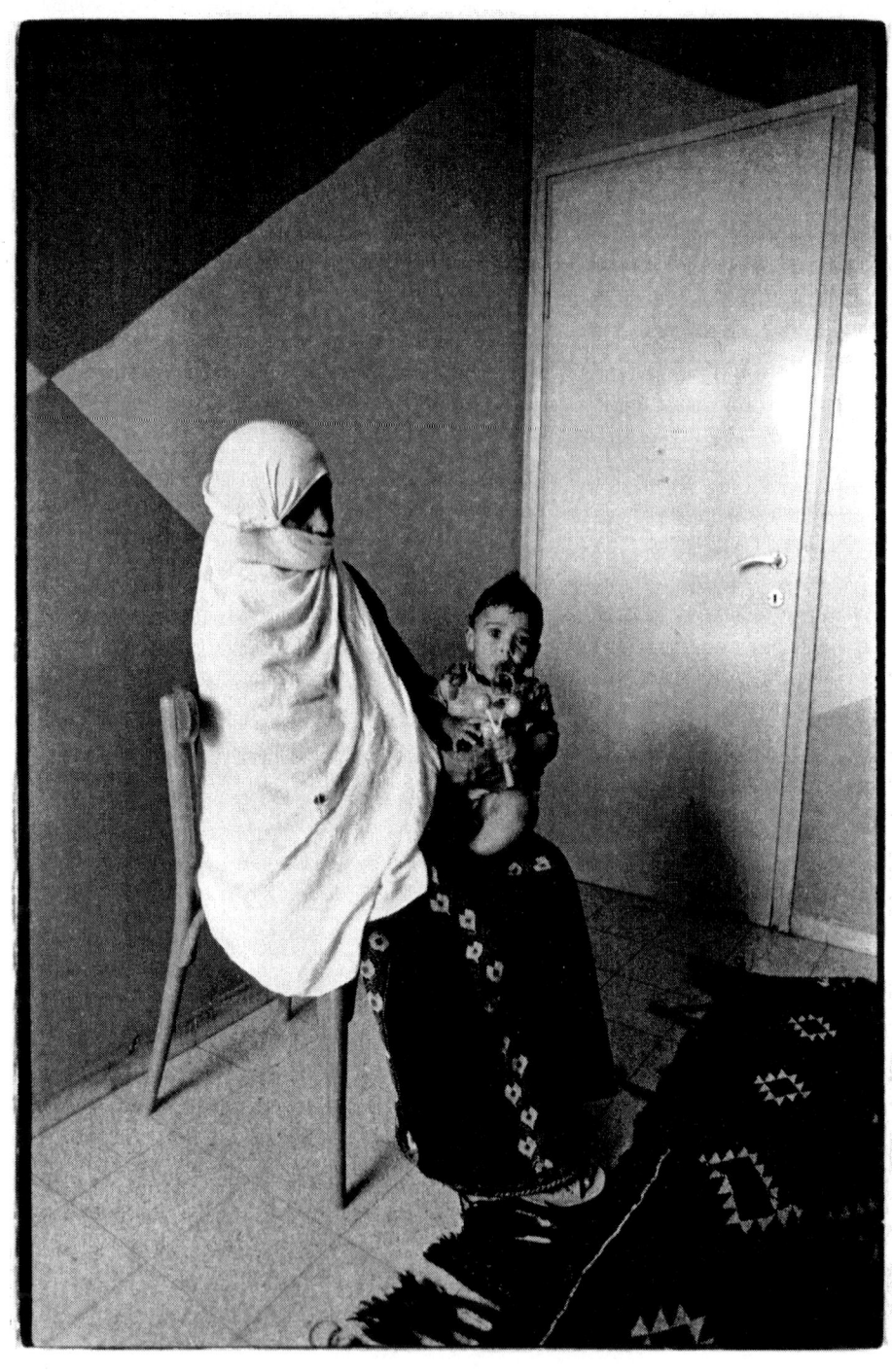

Figure 5. Bedouin woman with a child

Figure 6. Bedouin encampment

Figure 7. Beersheba 1979, near a Bedouin encampment

Figure 8. A flat in the old city

Figure 9. Mrs. Farraj

NOTES

1. Edward Said, "The Mirage of Peace," *The Nation* 16 Oct. 1995: 420.

2. Mary Price, *The Photograph: A Strange Confined Space* (Stanford: Stanford UP, 1994) 117.

3. Linda Hutcheon, *The Politics of Postmodernism* (London and New York: Routledge. 1989) 3.

4. Edward Said, "Ground Realities of a Palestine where Arabs and Jews Coexist," *The Asian Age* 1 Dec. 1999: 13.

5. Edward Said, *After the Last Sky: Palestinian Lives* (New York: Pantheon, 1986) 16–17.

6. Said believes that a demand for a truly Palestinian entity is unforeseeable today. Nor can the Israelis deny the existence of Palestinians —no matter how many check-points, roads, and fences Barak and his advisers keep inventing. The fact is that neither Palestinians, nor the Jews can be made distant from each other. The dreams of a pure and uncontaminated statehood for both communities are now not possible or practical. See Edward Said, "Ground Realities of a Palestine where Arabs and Jews Coexist," *The Asian Age* 1 Dec. 1999: 13.

7. Said's text is accompanied by photographs taken by Jean Mohr.

8. Edward Said, *After the Last Sky: Palestinian Lives* (New York: Pantheon, 1986) 6.

9. Linda Hutcheon, *The Politics of Postmodernism* (London and New York: Routledge, 1989) 120–121.

10. Linda Hutcheon, *The Politics of Postmodernism* (London and New York: Routledge, 1989) 130–131.

11. Edward Said, *After the Last Sky: Palestinian Lives* (New York: Pantheon, 1986) 12.

12. Edward Said, *After the Last Sky: Palestinian Lives* (New York: Pantheon, 1986) 26.

13. Edward Said, *After the Last Sky: Palestinian Lives* (New York: Pantheon, 1986) 84.

14. Edward Said, *After the Last Sky: Palestinian Lives (New York: Pantheon, 1986)* 142.

15. Edward Said, *Peace and its Discontents* (New York: Vintage, 1996) XXXV.

16. Edward Said, *Out of Place: A Memoir* (New York: Alfred Knopf, 1999) : 295.

Epilogue

The world knows us by our faces, the most naked, the most vulnerable, exposed
and significant topography of the body. When our *caras* do not live up to the
"image" that the family or community wants us to wear and when we rebel against
the engraving of our bodies, we experience ostracism, alienation, isolation, and
shame . . . .Some of us are forced to acquire the ability, like a chameleon, to
change color when the dangers are many and the options few. Some of us who
already "wear many changes/inside of our skin" (Audre Lorde) have been forced to
adopt a face that would pass . . . ."Over my mask is your mask of me." (Mitsuye
Yamada) These masking roles exact a toll . . . [1]

Forms of impersonation and masquerade are of course integral to the symbolic
repertoire of all the peoples of the world. The mask has a long cultural history
associated with ritual and performance. Masks seem to . . . help people to cope
with . . ."the metaphysics of ambivalence . . ."[2]

I too wear masks. I too masquerade. Yet, *all my masks are not masquerades.* As I
re-write this book at a different time and on a different continent, I am struck by
the myriad masks I, too, am compelled to wear. The mechanism of masking and
masquerade elaborated in the previous chapters suggest a remarkable degree of
versatility and usefulness that accompanies this concept, particularly for the
understanding of the pluralities of the postcolonial situation, *both* in their private
and public manifestations.

This book is an attempt, then, to *understand* both the public and private
agonies of masquerading. However, it also opens up cracks and fissures within the
process of masking—its *interfaces*— that could provide spaces for resistance. For,
postcolonial masquerade, as I have indicated in my reading of diverse texts, is the
locus where multiple mediations of gender, sexuality, race, and ethnicity, intersect,
interact and are enunciated. Masquerade is a powerful metaphor through which we
can understand both the material and aesthetic strategies of varied postcolonial

119

texts and discourses. The trope permits a critical re-examination of the predicaments of postcolonial identities and dislocations in an increasingly aggressive, neocolonial global world. At the same time it contains within it notions of *changeability* , *metamorphosis*, and *contradiction*. These are the dynamics of masquerade that also offer possibilities of subversion. This book is an attempt to think critically about a theoretical concept that translates itself into material praxis.

The dynamics of masquerade represented here reflect both the anxieties and the freedoms of postcolonial life. Moreover, masquerade implies a creative transformation of theoretical and political questions of postcoloniality into aesthetic practices that destabilize dominant notions of identity formations or unveil the problematics and anxieties of representing complex experiences of postcoloniality like nationhood, exile, and history.

My own interest stems from the myriad effects and affects of masquerade both in its private and public manifestations. It's practical applications, as in the case of Parmar's films de-academize theory by forging a link between community and the academy. In its private applications, as in the case of Said's photographic essay, masquerade opens up spaces for a poetic/political/personal discussion of "internal exile". In its creative manifestation, as in the case of Kureishi's films, it develops aesthetic strategies that resist dominant cultural practices, by both celebrating and politicizing pleasure and articulating new positions of "in-betweeness." And, in its anxious and uncertain moments, as in the case of Rushdie's novel, masquerade wavers between affirmation and negation in it's attempt to re-write history in the name of the woman.

To wear masks, however, doesn't always indicate masquerade. We wear masks to conceal, we masquerade to conceal and reveal. Through masquerade we enter new terrains, make new faces— in the words of Gloria Anzaldua, "To make face is to have face—dignity and self respect'. (*Making Face*, xxvii). It is through art and activism, and expression that masquerade displaces and replaces memories. It is through masquerade that we can understand and critique the world we live in.

My own investigation is informed by the contradictory, representational, and performative nature of masquerade. Resituated and remade in different contexts, its protean qualities delink it from its originary conceptions and permit us to re-negotiate or reexamine valuable cultural, political, theoretical, and artistic texts within the context of a globalized postcolonial world.

In the exigencies of both political and personal struggles that characterize the "New World order", masquerade is an idiom available for the oppressed and the uprooted, the estranged, or the marginalized, to express and shape identities and communities. However its ability to duplicate and deceive are also embedded within its dynamics. This book has been an attempt to present the possibilities and ramifications of such an idiom.

NOTES

1. Gloria Anzaldua, ed. *Making Face, Making Soul: Haciendo Caras* (San Francisco: Aunt Lute, 1990) xv.

2. Sumita Chakravarty. *National Identity in Indian Popular Cinema: 1947–1987* (Delhi: Oxford UP, 1996) 6.

Bibliography

Ahmad, Aijaz. *In Theory: Classes, Nations, Literatures*. London: Verso, 1992.

Ahmad, Akbar. *Pakistan Society: Islam, Ethnicity, and Leadership in South Asia*. Karachi: Oxford UP, 1986.

Alloula, Malek. *The Colonial Harem*. Minneapolis: U of Minnesota P, 1986.

Amin, Samir. *Class and Nation*. London: Monthly Review P, 1971.

———. *Imperialism and Unequal Development*. New York: Monthly Review P, 1977.

Anderson, Benedict. *Imagined Communities: Reflections on the Origins and Spread of Nationalism*. London: Verso, 1983.

Anderson, Perry. *English Questions*. London and New York: Verso, 1992.

Anzaldua, Gloria. *Borderlands, La Frontera: The New Mestiza*. San Francisco: Aunt Lute, 1987.

———, ed. *Making Face, Making Soul: Haciendo Caras*. San Francisco: Aunt Lute, 1990.

Appiah, Kwame Anthony. "Is the Post-in Postmodernism the Post—in Postcolonialism?" *Critical Inquiry* 17.2 (1992) : 336–357.

Appiganesi, Lisa and Sara Maitland, eds. *The Rushdie File*. Syracuse: Syracuse UP, 1990.

Apter, Emily. *Feminizing the Fetish*. Ithaca: Cornell UP, 1991.

Ashcroft, Bill, Gareth Griffiths, and Helen Tiffin. *The Empire Writes Back: Theory and Practice in Post Colonial Literature*. London: Routledge, 1989.

———, eds. *The Post-Colonial Studies Reader*. London and New York: Routledge, 1995.

Bakhtin, Mikhail. *The Dialogic Imagination*. Austin: U of Texas P, 1981.

———. *Speech Genres and Other Late Essays*. Trans. Vern McGee. Austin: U of Texas P, 1986.

Bannerjee, Diptendra. *Marxian Theory and the Third World*. N. Delhi: Stage Publications, 1985.

Barker, Francis, ed. *Europe and its Others*. Colchester: U of Essex P, 1985.

Barthes, Roland. *The Pleasure of the Text*. New York: Hill and Wang, 1975.

———. Camera Lucida: *Reflections on Photography*. New York: Hill and Wang, 1981.

Bhabha, Homi. *The Location of Culture*. London and New York: Routledge, 1994.

———, ed. *Nation and Narration*. London and New York: Routledge, 1990.

———, "Of Mimicry and Man: The Ambivalence of Colonial Discourse," *October* 28 (1984) : 125-133.

———, "Race and the Humanities: The 'Ends' of Modernity?" *Public Culture* 4.2 (1992) : 81-85.

———, "Signs Taken as Wonders: Questions of Ambivalence and Authority Under a Tree Outside Delhi, May 1817," *Critical Inquiry* 12.1 (1985) 144-65.

———, "The World and the Home." *Social Text* 31/32 (1992) : 141-153.

Bolton, Richard, ed. *The Contest of Meaning: Critical Histories of Photography*. Cambridge, MIT P, 1993.

Bordwell, David. *Narration in the Fiction Film*. Madison: U of Wisconsin P, 1985.

Brantlinger, Patrick. *Rule of Darkness: British Literature and Imperialism*. Ithaca: Cornell UP, 1988.

———. *Crusoe's Footprints: Cultural Studies in Britain and America*. New York: Routledge, 1990.

Brenan, Timothy. *Salman Rushdie and the Third World: Myths of the Nation*. New York: St. Martin's P, 1989.

Bristow, Joseph. "Being Gay: Politics, Identity, Pleasure." *New Formations* 9. (1989) : 61-82.

Burgin, Victor, James Donald, and Cora Kaplan, eds. *Formations of Fantasy*. London: Routledge, 1986.

Burgin, Victor. *The End of Art Theory: Criticism and Postmodernity*. Atlantic Highlands, NJ: Humanities P International, 1986.

———, ed. *Thinking Photography*. London: Macmillan, 1982.

Butler, Judith. *Gender Trouble: Feminism and the Subversion of Identity*. New York: Routledge, 1990.

Butler, Judith, and Joan Scott, eds. *Feminists Theorize the Political*. New York and London: Routledge, 1992.

Carby, Hazel. *Reconstructing Womanhood*. Oxford: Oxford UP, 1987.

Carson, Diane, Linda Dittmar, and Janice Welsch, eds. *Multiple Voices in Feminist Film Criticism*. Minneapolis: U of Minnesota P, 1994.

Case, Sue Allen, ed. *Performing Feminisms: Feminist Theory And Theater.* Baltimore: Johns Hopkins, 1990.

Castle, Terry. *Masquerade and Civilization.* Stanford: Stanford UP, 1986.

Center for Contemporary Cultural Studies. *The Empire Strikes Back: Race and Racism in 70's* Britain. London: Hutchinson, 1982.

Cesaire, Aime. *Discourse on Colonialism.* New York: Monthly Review P, 1972.

Chakrabarty, Dipesh. "Postcoloniality and the Artifice of History: Who Speaks for 'Indian' Pasts?" *Representations* 32 (1992) : 1–25.

Chakravarty, Sumita. *National Identity in Indian Popular Cinema 1947–1987.* Delhi: Oxford UP, 1996.

Cham, M., and C. Andrade-Watkins, eds. *Blackframes: Critical Perspectives on Black Independent Cinema.* Cambridge : MIT P, 1988.

Chatterjee, Partha. *Nationalist Thought and the Colonial World.* London: Zed, 1986.

Chomsky, Noam. *The Fateful Triangle.* Boston: South End P, 1983.

Christian, Barbara. "The Race for Theory." *Cultural Critique* 6 (1987) : 51–63.

Cook, Pam and Philip Dodd, eds. *Women and Film: A Sight and Sound Reader.* Philadelphia: Temple UP, 1993.

Crimp, Douglas. "The Photographic Activity of Postmodernism." *October* 15 (1980) : 91–101.

Daniels, Therese, and Jane Gerson, eds. *The Color Black: Black Images in British Television.* London: BFI, 1989.

Davis, Angela. *Women, Race and Class.* New York: Vintage, 1983.

Davis, R.C., ed. *Lacan and Narration: The Psychoanalytic Difference in Narrative Theory.* Baltimore: Johns Hopkins, 1983.

De Lauretis, Teresa. *Alice Doesn't: Feminism, Semiotics, Cinema.* Bloomington: Indiana UP, 1984.

———. *Feminist Studies/Critical Studies.* Bloomington: Indiana UP, 1986.

———. *Technologies of Gender: Essays on Theory, Film and Fiction.* Bloomington: Indiana UP, 1987.

Derrida, Jacques. *Dissemination.* Chicago: Chicago UP, 1981.

———. *Of Grammatology.* Baltimore: Johns Hopkins, 1976.

———. *Writing and Difference.* Chicago: U of Chicago P, 1978.

Dingwaney, Anuradha and Carol Maier. *Between Languages and Cultures: Translation and Cross-cultural Texts.* Delhi: Oxford UP, 1996.

Dirlik, Arif. "The Postcolonial Aura: Third World Criticism in the Age of Global Criticism." *Critical Inquiry* 20.2 (1994) : 328–356.

Djebar, Assia. *Fantasia: An Algerian Cavalcade.* Portsmouth: Heinemann, 1993.

Doane, Mary Ann. *Femmes Fatales: Feminism, Film Theory, Psychoanalysis.* New York: Routledge, 1991.

———. *The Desire to Desire: Women's Film of the 1940's.* Bloomington: Indiana UP, 1987.

During, Simon, ed. *The Cultural Studies Reader.* New York and London: Routledge, 1993.

Eagleton, Terry and Edward Said. *Nationalism, Colonialism and Literature.* Minneapolis; U of Minnesota P, 1990.

Ellis, John. *Visible Fictions: Cinema, Television, Video.* London: Routledge, 1982.

Essays by Arab and Muslim Writers in defense of Free Speech. *For Rushdie.* New York: George Braziller, 1993.

Fanon, Frantz. *Black Skin, White Masks.* New York: Grove, 1967.

———. *The Wretched of the Earth.* New York: Grove, 1965.

Felman, Shoshana. *Jacques Lacan and the Adventure of Insight: Psychoanalysis in Contemporary Culture.* Cambridge: Harvard UP, 1987.

Ferguson, Russell, et al, eds. *Out There: Marginalization and Contemporary Cultures.* Cambridge: MIT P, 1990.

———, et al, eds. *Discourses: Conversations in Postmodern Art and Culture.* Cambridge: MIT P, 1990.

Fischer, Michael and Mehdi Abedi. *Debating Muslims* Madison: U of Wisconsin P, 1990.

Foster, Hal, ed. *The Anti Aesthetic: Essays in Postmodern Cultures.* Seattle: Bay P, 1983.

———, ed. *Vision and Visuality* Seattle: Bay P, 1988.

Foucault, Michel. *The Archaeology of Knowledge.* New York: Pantheon, 1972.

——— *The History of Sexuality.* Vol. 1. New York: Pantheon, 1978.

Franklin, Sarah, Celia Lury, and Jackie Stacey, eds. *Off-Center: Feminism and Cultural Studies.* London: Harper Collins Academic, 1991.

Fuss, Diana. *Essentially Speaking: Feminism, Nature and Difference.* New York: Routledge, 1989.

Gaines, Jane, and Charlotte Herzog, eds. *Fabrications: Costume and the Female Body* New York: Routledge, 1990.

Gallop, Jane. *Reading Lacan.* Ithaca: Cornell UP, 1985.

Garber, Marjorie. *Vested Interests: Cross-Dressing and Cultural Anxiety.* New York: Routledge, 1992.

Gates, Henry Louis, ed. *Race, Writing, and Difference.* Chicago: U of Chicago P, 1986.

Gellner, E. Nations and Nationalism. Oxford: Basil Blackwell, 1983.

Gever, Martha, John Greyson, and Pratibha Parmar, eds. Queer Looks: Perspectives on Lesbian and Gay Film and Video. New York and London: Routledge, 1993.

Gilroy, Paul. Small Acts: Thoughts on the Politics of Black Cultures. New York: Serpent's Tail, 1993.

———. There Ain't No Black in the Union Jack. London: Hutchinson, 1987.

Goldberg, David, ed. Anatomy of Racism. Minneapolis: U of Minnesota P, 1990.

Gramsci, Antonio. Selections from the Prison Notebooks. New York: International Publishers, 1971.

———. Selections from Political Writings. New York: International Publishers, 1977.

———. Selections from Cultural Writings. Cambridge: Harvard UP, 1991.

Grossberg, Lawrence, Cary Nelson, and Paula Treichler, eds. Cultural Studies. New York and London: Routledge, 1992.

Grosz, Elizabeth. Jacques Lacan: A Feminist Introduction. London: Routledge, 1989.

Guha, Ranajit and Gayatri Chakravorty Spivak, eds. Selected Subaltern Studies. New York: Oxford UP, 1988.

Gurr, Andrew. Writers in Exile: The Identity of Home in Modern Literature. Brighton: Harvester, 1981.

Hall, Stuart. The Hard Road to Renewal: Thatcherism and the Crisis on the Left. London and New York: Verso, 1988.

Hall, Stuart and Tony Jefferson, eds. Resistance Through Rituals: Youth Subcultures in Post War Britain. London: Harper Collins Academic, 1976.

Hamilton, Ian. "The First Life of Salman Rushdie." New Yorker Dec. 25 and Jan. 1. 1996: 90–113.

Harasym, Sara, ed. The Post-Colonial Critic: Interviews, Strategies, Dialogues. New York: Routledge, 1990.

Haraway, Donna. Primate Visions: Gender, Race and Nature in the World of Modern Science. New York: Routledge, 1989.

Harris, Wilson. The Womb of Space: The Cross-Cultural Imagination. Westport: Greenwood, 1983.

Hebdige, Dick. Subculture: The Meaning of Style. New York: Routledge, 1979.

Hiro, Dilip. Black British White British: A History of Race Relations in Britain. London: Paladin, 1992.

Hobsbawm, Eric. The Age of Empire. New York: Random House, 1987.

Hogan, Patrick Colm and Lalita Pandit, eds. *Literary India: Comparative Studies in Aesthetics, Colonialism and Culture.* New York: State U of New York P, 1995.

Hood, Stuart, ed. *Behind the Screens: British Television in the Nineties.* London: Lawrence and Wishart, 1994.

hooks, bell. *Ain't I a Woman: Black Women and Feminism.* Boston: South End P, 1981.

————. *Feminist Theory: From Margin to Center.* Boston: South End P, 1984.

————. *Talking Back.* Boston: South End P, 1989.

————. *Yearning: Race, Gender and Cultural Politics.* Boston: South End P, 1990.

————. *Reel to Real: Race, Sex and Class at the Movies.* London and New York: Routledge, 1996.

Hooks, bell and Cornell West. *Breaking Bread: Insurgent Black Intellectual Life.* Boston: South End P, 1991.

Hutcheon, Linda. *A Poetics of Postmodernism: History, Theory, Fiction.* New York and London: Routledge, 1988.

————. *The Politics of Postmodernism.* London and New York: Routledge, 1989.

Huyssen, Andreas. *Modernism, Mass Culture, and Postmodernism.* London: Macmillan, 1986.

Institute of Contemporary Art. *Black Film, British Cinema.* London: BFI, 1988.

————. *Identity: The Real Me.* London: BFI, 1987.

Jameson, Fredric. *The Political Unconscious: Narrative as a Socially Symbolic Act.* Ithaca: Cornell UP, 1981.

————. *Postmodernism or the Logic of Late Capitalism.* Durham: Duke UP. 1991.

Jan Mohamed, Abdul R., and David Lloyd, eds. *The Nature and Context of Minority Discourse.* New York: Oxford UP, 1990.

Jayawardena, Kumari, ed. *Feminism and Nationalism in the Third World.* London: Zed, 1986.

Kaleta, Kenneth. Hanif Kureishi: *Postcolonial Storyteller.* Austin: U of Texas P, 1998.

Katrak, Ketu. "Decolonizing Culture: Toward a Theory for Postcolonial Women's Texts." *Modern Fiction Studies* 35.1 (1989) : 157–179.

Kauffman, Linda, ed. *Gender and Theory: Dialogues on Feminist Criticism.* New York: Basil Blackwell, 1989.

Kristeva, Julia. "Women's Time." *Signs* 7.1 (1981) : 5–35.

Kruger, Barbara, and Phil Mariani, eds. *Remaking History.* Seattle: Bay P, 1989.

Krupnik, Mark, ed. *Displacement: Derrida and After.* Bloomington: Indiana UP, 1983.

Kureishi, Hanif. *The Black Album.* New York: Scribner, 1995.

———. *The Buddha of Suburbia.* New York: Viking, 1990.

———. *London Kills Me.* London: Penguin, 1984.

———. *My Beautiful Laundrette.* London: Penguin, 1984.

———. *Outskirts.* London: Riverrun P, 1983.

———. *Sammy and Rosie Get Laid.* London: Penguin, 1988.

Lacan, Jacques. *Ecrits.* London: Tavistock, 1977.

———. *Feminine Sexuality.* New York: Norton, 1982.

———. *The Four Fundamental Concepts of Psychoanalysis.* London: Hogarth P, 1977.

Lacapra, Dominick, ed. *The Bounds of Race.* Ithaca: Cornell UP, 1991.

Laclau, Ernesto. *Politics and Ideology in Marxist Theory.* London: New Left Books, 1977.

Laclau, Ernesto and Chantal Mouffe. *Hegemony and Socialist Strategy: Towards a Radical Democratic Politics.* London: Verso, 1985.

Lamming, George. *The Pleasures of Exile.* London: Allison and Busby, 1960.

Landry, Donna, and Gerald Maclean, eds. *The Spivak Reader.* New York and London: Routledge, 1996.

Lemaire, Anika. *Jacques Lacan.* London: Routledge, 1977.

Liddle, Joanna and Rama Joshi. *Daughters of Independence: Gender, Caste, and Class in India.* London: Zed, 1986.

Loomba, Ania. *Colonialism/Postcolonialism.* London and New York: Routledge, 1998.

Lowe, Lisa. *Critical Terrains: French and British Orientalisms.* Ithaca: Cornell UP, 1991.

Lynch, Caitrin. "Nation, Woman, and the Indian Bourgeoisie: An Alternative Formulation." *Public Culture* 13 (1994) : 425–437.

Lyotard, Jean-Francois. *The Postmodern Condition: A Report on Knowledge.* Minneapolis: U of Minnesota P, 1984.

Mac Canell, Judith Flower. *Figuring Lacan: Criticism and the Cultural Unconscious.* Lincoln: U of Nebraska P, 1986.

Mani, Lata. "Contentious Traditions: The Debate on Sati in Colonial India." *Cultural Critique* 7 (1987) : 152–163.

Mannoni, O. *Prospero and Caliban: The Psychology of Colonization.* Ann Arbor: U of Michigan P, 1990.

Maranca, Bonnie, and Gautam Dasgupta, eds. *Interculturalism and Performance*. New York: PAJ Publications, 1991.

Mazrui, Ali. *Cultural Forces in World Politics*. London: Heinemann, 1990.

McCabe, Colin, ed. *High Theory, Low Culture: Analyzing Popular Television and Film*. New York: St. Martin's P, 1986.

McGee, Patrick. *Telling the Other: The Question of Value in Modern and Postcolonial Writing*. Ithaca: Cornell UP, 1992.

McGowan, John. *Postmodernism and Its Critics*. Ithaca: Cornell UP, 1991.

McRobbie, Angela. "Strategies of Vigilance: An Interview with Gayatri Chakravarty Spivak." *Block* 10 (1985) : 5–9.

Mellencamp, Patricia. *Indiscretions: Avant Garde Film, Video, and Feminism*. Bloomington: Indiana UP, 1990.

Memmi, Albert. *The Colonizer and the Colonized*. Boston: Beacon P, 1965.

Mercer, Kobena. "Black Hair/Style Politics." *New Formations* 3 (1987) : 33–54.

Michelson, Annette, et al, eds. October: *The First Decade, 1976–1986*. Cambridge, MIT P, 1987.

Mitchell, Juliet. *Psychoanalysis and Feminism*. New York: Viking, 1974.

Minh-Ha, Trinh. *Framer Framed*. New York and London: Routledge, 1992.

———. *When the Moon Waxes Red*. New York: Routledge, 1991.

———. *Woman, Native, Other*. Bloomington: Indiana UP, 1989.

Mohanty, Chandra Talpade, Ann Russo, and Lourdes Torres, eds. *Third World Women and the Politics of Feminism*. Bloomington: Indiana UP, 1991.

Mulvey, Laura. *Visual and Other Pleasures*. Bloomington: Indiana UP, 1989.

Naficy, Hamid. *Home, Exile, Homeland: Film, Media, and the Politics of Place*. New York and London: Routledge, 1999.

Naipaul, V.S. *The Mimic Men*. London: Penguin, 1976.

Nairn, Tom. *The Break-Up of Britain*. London: Verso, 1981.

Nandy, Ashish. *The Intimate Enemy: Loss and Recovery of Self Under Colonialism*. New York: Oxford UP, 1983.

Nichols, Bill. *Ideology and the Image*. Bloomington: Indiana UP, 1981.

Nicholson, Linda, ed. *Feminism/Postmodernism*. New York: Routledge, 1990.

Niranjana, Tejaswini. *Siting Translation: History, Post- Structuralism and the Colonial Context*. Berkeley: U of California P, 1992.

O'Hanlon, Rosalind. "Recovering the Subject: Subaltern Studies and the Histories of Resistance in Colonial South Asia." *Modern Asian Studies* 22.1 (1988) : 189–224.

Parker, Andrew, et al, eds. *Nationalisms and Sexualities*. New York and London: Routledge, 1992.

Parmar, Pratibha. "Hateful Contraries: Media Images of Asian Women." *Ten-8* 16 (1984) : 71–78.

———. "Other Kinds of Dreams." *Feminist Review* 31 (1989) : 55–66.

Parmar, Pratibha, and Valerie Amos. "Challenging Imperial Feminism." *Feminist Review* 17 (1984) : 3–19.

Parry, Benita. "Problems in Current Theories of Colonial Discourse." *Oxford Literary Review* 9 (1987) : 27–58.

———. "Signs of Our Times: A Discussion of Homi Bhabha's The Location of Culture." *Third Text* 28/29 (1994) : 5–24.

Penley, Constance, ed. *Feminism and Film Theory.* New York and London: Routledge, 1988.

Pines, Jim and Paul Willemen, eds. *Questions of Third Cinema.* London: BFI, 1989.

Price, Mary. *The Photograph: A Strange, Confined Space.* Stanford: Stanford UP, 1994.

Radhakrishnan, R. "Edward Said's Culture and Imperialism: A Symposium." *Social Text* 40 (1994) : 1–24.

Ragland-Sullivan, Ellie. *Jacques Lacan and the Philosophy of Psychoanalysis.* Urbana: U of Illinois P, 1986.

Rajan, Rajeswari Sunder. "The Subject of Sati: Pain and Death in the Contemporary Discourse on Sati." *Yale Journal of Criticism* 3.2 (1990) : 1–23.

Renov, Michael, ed. *Theorizing Documentary.* New York: Routledge, 1993.

Retmar, Roberto, Fernandez. *Caliban and Other Essays.* Minneapolis: U of Minnesota P, 1989.

Rose, Jacqueline. *Sexuality in the Field of Vision.* London: Verso, 1986.

Ross, Andrew. *Universal Abandon: The Politics of Postmodernism.* Minneapolis: U of Minnesota P, 1988.

Roudinesco, Elizabeth. *Jacques Lacan and Co.* Chicago: U of Chicago P, 1990.

Rushdie, Salman. *Imaginary Homelands.* London: Granta, 1991.

———. *Midnight's Children.* New York: Penguin, 1991.

———. *The Moor's Last Sigh.* London: Jonathan Cape, 1995.

———. *The Satanic Verses.* New York: Viking, 1988.

———. *Shame.* New York: Vintage, 1989.

Ryan, Michael. *Politics and Culture.* Baltimore: Johns Hopkins, 1989.

———. *Marxism and Deconstruction.* Baltimore: Johns Hopkins, 1984.

Ryan, Michael and Douglas Kellner. *Camera Politica: The Politics and Ideology of Contemporary Hollywood Film.* Bloomington: Indiana UP, 1988.

Saadawi, Nawal, El. *The Hidden Face of Eve: Women in the Arab World.*
    Boston: Beacon P, 1980.
Said, Edward. *After the Last Sky: Palestinian Lives.* New York: Routledge, 1986.
———. *Covering Islam.* New York: Pantheon, 1981.
———. *Culture and Imperialism.* New York: Alfred Knoph, 1993.
———. "Ground Realities of a Palestine Where Arabs and Jews Coexist." *The
    Asian Age* Dec. 1 1999 : 13.
———. "The Mirage of Peace." *The Nation* Oct. 16. 1995 : 413–420.
———. *Orientalism.* New York: Random House, 1979.
———. *Out of Place: A Memoir.* New York: Alfred Knopf, 1999.
———. *Peace and its Discontents.* New York: Vintage, 1996.
———. *The Question of Palestine.* New York: Times Books, 1979.
———. *Representations of the Intellectual.* New York: Pantheon, 1994.
———. "Representing the Colonized: Anthropology and its Interlocutors." *Critical
    Inquiry* 15.2 (1989) : 205–225.
———. *The World, the Text, and the Critic.* Cambridge: Harvard UP, 1983.
———. "The Undercurrents of Arafatism." *The Asian Age* Oct. 4, 1999 : 12.
Said, Edward and Christopher Hitchens, eds. *Blaming the Victims: Spurious
    Scholarship and the Palestinian Question.* London: Verso, 1988.
Sangari, Kum Kum. "The Politics of the Possible." *Cultural Critique* 7 (1987) :
    157–186.
Sangari, Kum Kum, and Sudesh Vaid, eds. *Recasting Women: Essays in Colonial
    History.* New Brunswick: Rutgers UP, 1990.
Schulte, Rainer, and John Biguenet, eds. *Theories of Translation: An Anthology
    from Dryden to Derrida.* Chicago: U of Chicago P, 1992.
Soja, Edward W. *Postmodern Geographies: The Reassertion of Space in Critical
    Social Theory.* New York: Verso, 1989.
Sontag, Susan. *On Photography.* New York: Anchor Books, 1977.
Spelman, Elizabeth. *Inessential Woman: Problems of Exclusion in Feminist
    Thought.* Boston: Beacon P, 1988.
Spivak, Gayatri Chakravorty. "Can the Subaltern Speak?" *Marxism and the
    Interpretation of Culture.* Eds. Cary Nelson and Lawrence Grossberg.
    Urbana: U of Illinois P, 1988. 271–313.
———. *A Critique of Postcolonial Reason: Toward a History of the Vanishing
    Present.* Calcutta: Seagull, 1999.
———. *In Other Worlds: Essays in Cultural Politics.* New York and London:
    Routledge, 1988.

—— *Imaginary Maps: Three Stories by Mahasweta Devi.* New York and London: Routledge, 1995.

——. "In Praise of Sammy and Rosie Get Laid." *Critical Quarterly* 31.2 (1989): 80–88.

——. *Outside in the Teaching Machine.* New York and London: Routledge, 1993.

Sprinker, Michael, ed. *Edward Said: A Critical Reader.* Cambridge: Basil Blackwell, 1992.

Stam, Robert. *Subversive Pleasures: Bakhtin, Cultural Criticism, and Film.* Baltimore: Johns Hopkins, 1989.

Suleri, Sara. *The Rhetoric of English in India.* Chicago: U of Chicago P, 1992.

——. "Woman Skin Deep: Feminism and the Postcolonial Condition." *Critical Inquiry* 18.4 (1992) : 756–769.

Thiong'o, Ngugi Wa. *Decolonizing the Mind: The Politics of Language in African Literature.* Portsmouth: Heinemann, 1986.

Tiffin, Chris, and Alan Lawson, eds. *De-Scribing Empire: Postcolonialism and Textuality.* London and New York: Routledge, 1994.

Turner, Graeme. *British Cultural Studies: An Introduction.* New York and London: Routledge, 1992.

Varadharajan, Asha. *Exotic Parodies: Subjectivity in Adorno, Said and Spivak.* Minneapolis: U of Minnesota P, 1995.

Vishwanathan, Gauri. *Masks of Conquest: Literary Study and British Rule in India.* New York: Columbia UP, 1989.

Volosinov, V.N. *Marxism and the Philosophy of Language.* New York and London: Seminar Press, 1973.

Williams, Raymond. *Resources of Hope.* London: Verso, 1989.

Yarbo-Bejarno, Yvonne. "The Female Subject in Chicano Theater: Sexuality, 'Race', and Class." *Theater Journal* 38.4 (1986) : 389–407.

Young, Robert. *White Mythologies: Writing History and the West.* New York: Routledge, 1990.

Zamora, Lois Parkinson and Wendy Faris, eds. *Magical Realism: Theory, History, Community.* Durham: Duke UP, 1995.

Zizek, Slavoj. *The Sublime Object of Ideology.* London: Verso, 1989.

Index